GW00870001

# SM/
# Money
## How To Create
## Financial Freedom

## Charlie Reading
## Charlotte Colton

WRITE BUSINESS RESULTS

This book was produced in collaboration with Write Business Results Ltd.

www.writebusinessresults.com info@writebusinessresults.com

ISBN-13: 978-1977901521

ISBN-10: 1977901522


First published in the United Kingdom in 2017 via CreateSpace

This book is designed to provide information that the author believes to be accurate on the subject matter it covers, but it is sold with the understanding that neither the authors nor the publisher is offering individualised advice tailored to any specific portfolio or to any individual's particular needs, or rendering investment advice or other professional services such as financial, legal or accounting advice. A competent professional's services should be sought if one needs expert assistance in areas that include investment, legal and accounting advice.

This publication references performance data collated over several years. Past results do not guarantee future performance. Additionally, performance data, in addition to laws and regulations, change over time, which could change the status of the information in this book. This book provides solely historical data to discuss and illustrate its underlying financial principles. Additionally, this book is not intended to serve as the basis for any financial decision, as a recommendation of a specific investment adviser, or as an offer to sell or purchase any security. Only a prospectus may be used to offer to sell or purchase securities, and a prospectus must be read and considered carefully before one invests or spends money.

For further information please visit www.efficientportfolio.co.uk

# Contents

# The Importance Of Preparing For Your Future

I sat, pinned to my chair, unable to move. I don't know if it was fear or something else, but my legs refused to function and I couldn't open my mouth. Being interrogated by a man who I can only describe as a goliath, was not how I thought I'd spend my afternoon. His booming voice cut through the stifling, smothering silence of the dark room like an axe. The throbbing vein in his temple looked like it was about to explode. His face was contorted into a pulsating grimace that made me dig my nails into my sweating palms.

I'd not felt this way since I was called into my headmaster's office for yet another school boy misdemeanour. But I had more to worry about than the wrath of my parents or teachers. This time, my future was on the line.

"I don't care if you don't sleep for a week, I want that money in my account now! I make the rules for this game, and right now you're on your last Get Out Of Jail Free card.

Time's up. I want the money."

After a painfully quiet pause, I somehow managed to squeak out a response; "I just don't think it's right. It's not fair to do this to those people."

"I don't pay you to think", he boomed. "I pay you to make me rich".

That was the final straw. Of all of the diabolical things I'd heard from this man, this was the end for me. I couldn't take it anymore. I had to get out. And I had to do it now.

My first day in the city was full of hope and excitement. I was finally here, ready to start my new life. The morning dew was sparkling on the windows of the tallest and most impressive skyscrapers I had ever seen; the countless pigeons seemed to coo in harmony, as if to welcome me to their marvellous city. London lay sprawled out in front of me, full of endless possibility and countless charm. This was my city for the taking.

Despite having travelled through numerous capitals all over the world, nowhere compares to London at 6am. The streets are coming alive with the hustle and bustle of traders and train drivers alike. The steam rising from the Thames shrouds the city in a wondrous cloak and the smell of the air feeds your soul with a sense of hunger, wealth and success.

Walking along streets that I had only ever seen in literature or on the Monopoly board at home made me feel like I was walking amongst giants. So many heroes, and villains, had trodden these same paths before me. I felt honoured to walk in their footsteps. But now I was going to be great; I was determined to become the next London legend.

Growing up as a farmer's son, I was used to hard work. Agriculture is a demanding business that consumes your time and tires your limbs. During harvest, sleep is not an option. But to reap what you sow takes commitment, dedication and sacrifice. These were lessons I learnt at a very young age from my father and his before him.

They say that farming is in your blood. But I don't think it was ever truly in mine. Whilst I knew that I needed to work hard for my future, I always had a feeling that my talents lay elsewhere. I love the bucolic beauty of the rural landscapes where I grew up, but farming the land just wasn't for me.

And this seed of feeling in my gut only grew as I got older. At 18 I did what all "good farmers' sons" do - I went to university to study agriculture. The problem was, the lure of the city - in this case Newcastle - held far more appeal than the rolling green hills of home. Every day I'd see the office workers dressed in immaculate tailoring, making their way to their desks. I wondered what they did, how they earned their keep and how exciting their lives must be.

So I ploughed on through university, doing enough to get me by but not a lot more. When I finished, I didn't have a plan, I just knew that I needed to find a different path in life that wasn't farming. I did the typically nineties thing of trying to find myself: I travelled to South East Asia and Australia and drank in the sights and sounds. Travel really does broaden your mind and I owe my life to it. It opened my eyes to new possibilities and showed me that the world really was my oyster.

But by the time me and my trusty backpack made it home, I was back to square one. Travelling had been amazing, but what now? I was back on the farm, helping Dad plough the fields, but not doing what I wanted.

Maybe it's the secret 'hippie' in me, having been allowed free roam on my travels, but I am a firm believer that life gives you what you need, when you need it. One damp day I had been given reprieve from the fields, so was sitting in my parent's front room; and then I saw it. An advert offering financial advice to farmers. This got me thinking. I was from farming stock, so I knew the market place well. I could help so many of my father's friends and family, if only I knew about finance.

So, that brings me to London. Where better to learn about money management than in one of the greatest financial centres of the world? Or so I thought.

From day one, I was very different to my colleagues. The exhilaration I had felt walking to work had melted into an unsettling sense of scepticism by lunchtime. The environment I found myself in can only be described as a cut-throat bear pit, where the red-tie wearing sales team fought it out to see who could make the most commission. They were hungry for fast-cars and bachelor pads on Butcher's Wharf, whereas I just wanted to help people.

My boss, who you've already met, used to impart some real pearls of wisdom. He'd order us to go out at the weekend and buy a Porsche, or put a deposit on a house we couldn't afford. His thinking was that if we needed money, we'd work tirelessly to get it. No matter what.

It's no surprise that the first image that springs to mind when you utter the words 'financial adviser' is that of an unscrupulous character, baying for your cash. The sad reality is that we were taught to be this stereotype. Pushing people into risky strategies, that could cost them their futures was our bread and butter. We were a greedy bunch, who'd sell short our own mothers to hit our sales targets.

And that's why I found myself in that chair, being berated by the 'Chief Bear'. I believed in the value of financial planning. Ethical, personal and tailored planning could genuinely help people to achieve their goals, but sadly, the environment I was in was purely motivated by self-gain.

I had to get out. And I had to do it now. I'd found my vocation and my voice. I stood up, shook his hand and left. For good. I was going to do the right thing and help people; not destroy their wealth for my own gain.

# Introduction

People often imagine financial advisers to be these Dick Turpin characters and admittedly, working in the world of finance people do frequently get the wrong first impression of who I am and why I do what I do. Sadly, the red tie-wearing, sales bell-dinging culture of some financial firms does still exist, as you've seen in the previous chapter. The truth is that there are some ruthless and immoral advisers out there and with stories like The Wolf Of Wall Street or Jerry Maguire, it's a perception of financial advisers that a lot of us might have had at one point or another.

I'm pleased to say that not everyone in my industry is a Ferrari driving, Saville-Row suit wearing highwayman, lining their hand-made Italian leather wallets with your hard-earned money, though. There are plenty of morally sound and well-intentioned financial advisers out there too. Working with upwards of 400 individuals and business owners who all want to be secure in their futures has taught me that if anything, there is too much different advice out there, rather than not enough or all bad.

We live in the information age and while this makes content readily available on any topic, it also means that the internet (and probably your inbox) is saturated with 'advice'. Advice on anything you could possibly dream of. It's all there at the click of a button, so how on earth are non-finance professionals supposed to be able to see the wood from the trees? If you've ever attempted online research into personal finance, you'll know first-hand the minefield I'm referring to.

While the convenience and accessibility of such information can be a blessing, when it comes to something as personal and important as your money - your future security, your home, the choices you make every day, your overall quality of life, possibly also the quality of your family's life - you should not have to go blindly through Google searching for half-baked answers from people you don't know or trust. Nor should you feel obliged to take advice from an adviser, accountant or anyone else on your finances before you feel confident in your decision-making.

Having observed the darker side of the financial world - the commission-hungry, sales-driven circle that might be behind some of this 'advice' - it is simply not worth the risk. Back in the early 2000s when I was new to personal finance and learned about the dangers out there, I quickly turned my back on that approach and set out to make a real difference instead. If you, too, are looking to improve your understanding of personal finance and gain clarity around what actions you need to take in order to create the future you want, you're in the right place.

I've found financial advice to be most helpful to others when it's given without expectation, and in a way that empowers the recipient to make their own decisions. I left the city because I didn't want to push people into products that weren't right for them, or force individuals to take too much risk with their money. I didn't want to profit from their demise; I wanted to help them profit from my expertise. That's why I left London and, for the second time in my life, headed back to the farm.

At this time, my wife Caryl and I wanted to start our own family, so moving out of the hustle and bustle of London and back into the peace and tranquillity of Rutland seemed like an idyllic plan. It was also my perfect opportunity to create a business that revolutionised financial planning.

After a couple of years of working under an umbrella firm, I finally took the leap and set up Efficient Portfolio in 2006. I left the skyscrapers of the city and established my own financial planning company in a renovated barn in the heart of the countryside. With my family's farming connections, this rural setting was the picture-perfect place to begin my journey. I could see that people outside The City needed my help as much, if not more, so that's where I began. My friendly and approachable version of financial planning sparked into life, and my true vocation took form.

It certainly wasn't an easy ride; anyone who has set up their own business will empathise with all of the trials, stresses and sleepless nights that filled my company's early days. But it was more than worth it.

Now I'm one of the top 10% of all financial planners in the country, my firm consistently wins national awards and I make my living by providing honest solutions that genuinely help people. But more than that, I have two beautiful daughters, who amaze me day after day; the most supportive wife in the world, whose creativity and sharp business sense has helped me build a company and lifestyle that changes people's lives; and a team, who share my values, and constantly strive to innovate and improve our firm to help better people's futures. I'm also fortunate to be surrounded by family and friends, and the gorgeous Rutland countryside, where you'll often spot me cycling, running or playing golf.

In my mind, I've found my slice of heaven, and it feels great! I want others to find theirs. Everyone can achieve their dreams, but sometimes you just need a helping hand. That's why I do what I do: my mission is to help others achieve their goals through clear and simple financial planning.

Drawing on over 15 years' experience in financial services, this book shows you how you can prepare yourself for the future you want, too. You'll learn actionable steps that you can implement today to become more in control and empowered by your personal finances. Using practical tools as well as industry insights and first-hand experiences, over the course of the next ninety minutes, I aim to provide you with a full understanding of what personal finance really is, why it matters, and how you can live the life you want.

So why is financial planning really so important? Surely, it's simple: you either have money, or you have to go out and make money. You either have it, or you don't. To an extent that's true, but the world of finance, like life, is not black and white. There is so much you can do to change your circumstances and improve what your future looks like. And now is the time to do it.

When I talk about the future, I often refer to retirement. In my mind, retirement is not about growing old and giving up. For me, retirement doesn't hold the connotations of something grey and bleak, it's the antithesis of that. Retirement is like a sparkling light on the horizon, full of hope and opportunities. My retirement will be full of excitement and adventure, where I will conquer Everest, dive to the depths of the oceans, and travel the world, embracing the diverse cultures that our wonderful planet has to offer. I'll spend time watching my grandkids grow and share my experiences with them and the generations to come. I'm going to live life to the full and love every moment of it. And money won't be a concern.

But I know that my version, or rather vision, of retirement is not shared by everyone. For millions, retirement is a scary prospect, full of uncertainty, worry and apprehension.

At the time of writing, the world I'm living in feels like it's hanging by a thread. Europe is at breaking point, America is in crisis and more generally, money is a huge concern to us all. Gone are the hedonistic days of the eighties when we received a good rate of return on our cash, and our investments were skyrocketing. Nowadays, it can feel like we get very little for our hard-earned money.

And then there's inflation decimating the cash we do have. We know we need to beat it, but the potential risks involved make this a highly unpalatable prospect. No-one wants to lose all of their money by investing in unsuitable and volatile environments. We're also living in a time where the aging population is becoming an increasing problem. In 2015, the population in the UK alone hit 65.1 million, the largest ever on record; in 2017, 17.8% of the populous is aged over 65 years old. With so many people to support, how can the State Pension provide more than a pittance? How will pensioners survive?

And that's just the tip of the iceberg: continually shifting pension legislation is confuddling the minds of even the savviest savers; ever-changing rules around tax stand to destroy the wealth we do manage to create, and don't even get me started on charges and penalties on old savings! The world of finance has become a confusing and complex beast, that is striking fear into so many of us.

A lot of people I talk to don't think that they will ever be able to afford to retire, and even more are just so perplexed by the financial landscape that they simply close their eyes and pray for the best. But avoidance is not the answer. Amid this chaos, you need to find some clarity and start to think about your future, not run away from it.

Now is the time to take action. If you don't, it might be too late. I've painted you a very grim picture of the 'apocalypse' ahead, but that only applies if you bury your head in the sand. Knowing your enemy will help you to prepare and overcome the potential pitfalls.

The problem is this: people don't plan ahead. This is a problem that myself and my firm, Efficient Portfolio, recognised a long time ago. We know that people desperately need to plan their finances, especially now, but are often left cold at the very thought of it. It might be that you have been burned by one of those dubious characters I've mentioned, or that you just don't see the point. Whether you're confused, scared or that the whole process seems too time consuming, I urge you to reconsider. But then again, if you're reading this, you've done the hard part: you've decided to take action.

I don't believe that financial planning is reserved for the elite. The company I've created empowers everyone and aims to deliver clear, concise planning built around you and your needs. You don't need to be a financial wizard to succeed in the current economic climate; instead, you just need some simple, honest guidance.

Financial planning is your most powerful retirement tool. If you want to build your wealth and protect your future, planning needs to be your weapon of choice. I know that financial planning will help you to overcome your concerns and help to deliver the exact future you want.

Efficient Portfolio was the first Chartered Financial Planning firm in my county. To achieve this accolade, myself and the team have invested our time into learning and training, culminating in an ongoing series of exams, constant development and rigorous adherence to regulations and ethics. Our development never stops; we never stop growing and advancing our knowledge. Our qualifications and desire to keep ahead of the rest, mean that we are placed within the top 7% of all firms in the UK.

You've probably got the impression that we do things a little differently to others; and we do! We pride ourselves on taking a revolutionary stance when it comes to financial planning. We don't talk about products or pigeon-hole people into strategies that might have historically worked. We talk about individuals and their needs, so that we can build unique planning that evolves and changes throughout a lifetime.

More importantly, we're normal people! Actually, I think we're extraordinary, but what I mean is that we communicate on your level, and explain financial planning in terms you can relate to. We love what we do, and our enthusiasm and commitment is infectious. We want you to feel as passionately about your future as we do.

In the remainder of this book, you're going to go on a journey into financial planning, where you're going to discover the exact steps you need to take to have a secure, financial future. Using my Efficient Money Method™, I will share the secrets to my own success, and that of my clients. Everything in this book has been explained in a clear-cut fashion, so that you can start planning now.

I'm so excited to share this with you. Your future starts now!

# Getting Prepared

*"Give me six hours to chop down a tree and I will spend the first four sharpening the axe"*

Abraham Lincoln

My entire career has been a voyage of discovery. Even when I was a novice and working in Biggsy's office, I began to learn about what it was people really need. Back then it often felt like we were pushing round people into square holes; we weren't asking them what they needed, but instead telling them what we wanted them to do.

After speaking with these clients day after day and hearing their concerns and fears, it soon dawned on me that we were missing a huge part of the puzzle. People don't want to be dictated to, they want to be empowered and they want to succeed in their own right. The reason why they want these things, is so that they have certainty and control over their own future.

Once that revelation had sunk in, I knew what I needed to do. Over the course of the next decade, I began to devour every piece of financial theory going. I set out to saturate my brain with the highest level of knowledge possible and answer this question: What do you need to do to be free? And more specifically, how can you be financially free?

Immersing myself in books, lectures, webinars and conferences certainly helped me on my journey. As did the rigorous exams required to become a Chartered Financial Planner. But the turning point for me was working with my clients. Understanding their needs and formulating solutions, not generating sales, enabled me to answer my question and create a system that anyone can use to become financially free. And this book will show you that exact system.

We all share several common goals in life: security, happiness and freedom. I'm certainly not going to tell you that money buys you all of these things, but it can help. The reality is that unless you take control of your financial future, you will be working until the day you die. You'll never be able to afford to move to your dream cottage in the countryside, or visit the majestic beauty of New Zealand. You won't have time to take day trips with your grandchildren to the seaside, or play a leisurely round of golf with your friends. You'll be stuck, working, struggling to put food on your table. Is that what you really want?

Some people enjoy what they do for a living and never want to give up, but is that you? If it is, wouldn't it more enjoyable still if you knew that working was a choice, and that you didn't have to do it if you didn't want to? Most people want to either stop work in the future, or have the choice to, and to be able to do that you need to create financial freedom; or enough capital that you can live off for the rest of your life.

These reasons and many more are why I created The Efficient Money Method™. The bottom line is that I want people to have a secure future through their finances, so they can live their lives with certainty and fill their years with the things they love. The Efficient Money Method is a unique system, built after years of work, which helps people plan for a financially fit, happy and healthy future.

On my journey through the financial world, I discovered that there are 6 key elements that need to be mastered if you want to create a financially free future. They are:

| 6 Key Elements | |
|---|---|
| Prepare | Plan |
| Profit | Pension |
| Progress | Personal |

These components work together to build your wealth, protect you against life's ups and downs and, crucially, keep you on track. Whilst the structure is the same for most people, the central purpose is unique for every individual. I don't believe that 'one size fits all'; we each have our own motivations, goals and needs. The Efficient Wealth Management Method holds your values at its core and tailors each area to fit around you. It's designed to help you fulfil your goals in a clear, understandable and accessible way.

This book centres on the first element of the Efficient Money Method, 'Prepare'. There are five other books too, to give you the full story, but the book you're reading right now specifically looks at how you can prepare for your future, starting now.

Before we go any further, a warning. If you already have financial freedom and know, with certainty, that you don't have to worry about what the future may hold, don't read on. Equally, if you believe that whatever you do, you'll never have enough, and you feel that your cash is safest under your mattress, chances are that you do not have the right mindset for what I'm about to tell you.

But if you want to learn how to better manage your money, achieve your goals and build a secure future, I can't wait to share The Efficient Money Method with you. You'll need to be prepared to make some changes, but the rewards you'll receive will be more than worth it.

One of my favourite quotes is 'You can always make money, but you can't always make memories.' A lot of people interpret the meaning of this as a warning not to worry about money; I see it in quite the opposite light. Spending time with your loved ones is the crux of happiness, but if you're working endless hours, how are you going to have any free time? The trick is to make your money work harder for you, not work excessively hard for your money. That's the ultimate goal and is how you will reach financial freedom. So how do you do that?

In 2016, I took part in the L'Etape Wales Dragon Ride in support of Macmillan Cancer Support and For Rutland In Rutland, an initiative to improve the lives of people living with long-term health conditions. If you're unfamiliar with this event, it's a 228km bike race through the beautiful, but merciless, Welsh mountains. I'd heard how tough it was, but, thriving on a challenge, in January 2016 I signed up. 6 months passed, but finally, on scorching hot day in June, me and 4999 other cyclists set off to conquer the undulating might of Wales.

But that's not the full story, is it? I didn't simply sign up in January and then turn up in June. If I had, there is no way I would have finished the race! I spent six months preparing: building my fitness, consulting bike specialists and adapting my diet to boost my performance. By the time June came around, I was in the best physical and mental condition I could be and felt ready to take on the challenge ahead.

We all understand that training for a sporting event will give us a far greater chance of finishing the race. But why don't we apply this logic to our finances? Surely, if you want to reach your goals, and be financially free, you need to train, you need to build up your strength, you need to prepare.

It will come as no great surprise that the first area of The Efficient Money Method is 'Prepare'. Whether you are 40 years from stopping work, or just 5, you need to get yourself into a position where you have every chance of being able to stop. This book shows you how to get your finances ready for financial freedom.

At the time of writing, the current State Pension in the UK is £159.55 a week. Do you think that this sum from the Government will provide you with a sufficient retirement income? Imagine trying to live your desired lifestyle on that amount of money. If you do not save enough for your retirement, that is what is going to end up happening to you. On the whole, the financial industry really isn't very good at teaching people the psychology, strategies or systems around saving, which are actually the fundamentals for your success. Only once you know these will you be able to prepare properly for your future.

In all credit to the Government, they have acknowledged that there is a huge problem with people not preparing, especially for their retirement. This explains why, in 2012, they started forcing people to save through company pension schemes. The rationale here being that if they can't teach people, they have to force them! One of the benefits of The Efficient Money Method is that it actually teaches you how to save; a skill you can pass on to the younger generations. It's my hope that through education, younger generations will be able to easily achieve their goals and not be faced with a bleak future. It will also help improve the chances for older people now, so the strategies I will explain are crucial to your success.

The 'Prepare' phase of The Efficient Money Method centres around 'The SMART Saving Solution', which ensures people are prepared for their retirement. This multifaceted solution is how me and my business, Efficient Portfolio,

have helped our clients build a money management system, so that they can ensure that they are saving the right
amounts for different areas of their life in a way that makes
the minimum impact on their lifestyle.

We want to ensure our clients have set into motion the
correct savings structures, understand how they can best
maximise their money, and also ensure they have a backup plan if something goes wrong, and we do that using
The SMART Saving Solution.

By saving in the right way now, you can ensure that you
will not become one of the 1.4 million people over 65 who
are still working. Instead, you will have the freedom to fill
your future with amazing experiences with those people
who are important to you, all the time knowing that your
savings are supporting you and giving you an enriched
life full of purpose and happiness.

The SMART Saving Solution ensures that you can retire
early enough to enjoy amazing experiences with your
friends and family, rather than listening to their stories of
freedom while you are still at work.

The next few chapters will look at The SMART Savings
Solution in depth, equipping you with all of the tools and
knowledge you need to prepare for your future freedom.

If you have any questions along the way, please contact
me on **hello@efficientportfolio.co.uk** and I would be more
than happy to help.

# ② Rationale

How would you feel if I told you that one simple act would help you to do everything you dreamt of? You'd do it, wouldn't you? Well, that act is very simple: saving is something that will enable you to live out your goals.

I will go on the assumption that you understand what I mean when I talk about 'saving'. To clarify, this is the act of putting money aside for a future event, project or pur chase. It's something that many of us want to do, but few actually achieve. Whilst the act of saving seems fairly simple, it's actually quite complex. Where and when you save your money, and how you do it, are somewhat of a grey area for most people, but understanding these areas will be the difference between working until you're 90 or clocking out at 50.

In the next chapter, we will look at exactly how and when to save, but before we get to that point, it's vital to understand what happens to your money when you save, and why you receive gains as well as losses. By understanding this you will have full control over your money, and know how to maximise the options available to you, which in turn will lead to a far healthier savings pot for the future.

The 'Rationale' of saving is the technical theory behind what factors impact upon the growth of your money. It's the 'inside knowledge' that will explain why some people make millions and others lose it all.

I'm sure many of you understand the difference between putting coppers in a jar at home and investing thousands in the Stock Market, but why are they different? They are both effectively modes of saving, but one seems safe and will generate no growth and the other appears risky, but could double, triple, even quadruple your money- or of course cost you everything.  But why does that happen?

I often find that the world of financial planning scares people to the point that they avoid it. When it comes to saving, I believe that this fear is born from their lack of understanding of how markets work, the impact interest and inflation has on the real value of their money, and how to safeguard themselves against threats. When I set out to create The Efficient Money Method, I wanted to share my knowledge and show people that with a little education, these areas are really nothing to be scared about.

There is a surreptitious power happening behind the scenes of saving, which can massively boost the returns you receive from your investments. It is a hidden force that increases the returns you get, however if you are un-aware of it, you might miss out. If you do, you'll have to save twice as hard to get the same results.

What am I talking about, you might be asking? When I say 'Rationale', I'm looking at four theories: Pound Cost Averaging, Compound Growth, Time in the Market and the Financial Freedom Number. This is the first aspect of 'Rationale': Pound Cost Averaging. To understand this, I want you to firstly consider this statement: 'Time in the market is more important than timing the market'.

Investing holds many negative connotations, mainly, in my view, because inexperienced investors have tried to guess when they should buy and when they should sell. This is when saving becomes risky. If you're trying to guess what investments will do well, and are constantly moving money around, not only will you get yourself into a tangle, you're likely to get burnt.

Even the notorious Warren Buffet, who has been given the moniker of 'the most successful investor in the world', has not always timed the market correctly. He even said, 'The only value of stock forecasters is to make fortune tellers look good'!

So, what's the solution? The trick is something called 'Pound Cost Averaging'.

People often assume that investing is a high-octane environment of 'buy, buy, buy' 'sell, sell, sell'. The very 80's image of caffeine fuelled, overly animated people shouting down huge mobile phones may be over 30 years behind us, but this type of investing does still exist; however, it is one I would strongly warn you against.

The problem with this strategy is that people try to 'time' the markets, by waiting until they change in their favour. They dip in and out of investing, trying to only purchase investments when they are doing well. The truth is, when investments are performing well they are expensive, because everyone wants them!

In October 2016, there was public outcry in the UK. One of the nation's most trusted supermarkets, Tesco, shocked consumers and left the average person distraught: they stopped selling Marmite! The reasons behind this were rooted in the post-Brexit performance of the pound against the euro, but the element of this story that piqued my interest was what happened with the few jars of Marmite that remained. Tesco were selling their scant supply of Marmite for £2.35, but canny eBay vendors, praying on the scarcity of one of UK's most beloved spreads, were advertising the same jar for a whopping £4 million!

I sincerely hope that no-one paid that much for a humble jar of Marmite, but it does illustrate what happens to price when suddenly everyone wants the same thing: the item that one day was low cost is suddenly inflated, meaning that you end up paying over the odds. If you had bought that jar of spread the day before 'Marmite-Gate' you would have paid a sensible price, but if you missed that day, you would be suddenly faced with an extortionate cost if you want a ticket on that train. In reality, people often miss the 'best days in the market' and end up paying over the odds for their sporadic investments, hence why we tend to steer clear of this investment strategy.

A better approach is to employ an ongoing strategy that means you don't miss out and don't pay over the odds. The strategy I'm proposing, which benefits from Pound Cost Averaging, means that you are continually invested in the market, so you never miss the best days or pay over the odds for your investments.

As an example, let's say that you save on a regular basis into a Self-Invested Pension Plan. Because you make regular contributions, you will be continually invested in the market, ensuring you don't miss out on the 'best days'. When prices are high you go against the grain and buy fewer units, but when prices are low, you buy more. This reduces the risk that you pay too much when the price is unusually high, and benefit from buying more when the price has fallen. This is Pound Cost Averaging.

In short, the investments you 'purchase' actually work out cheaper than if you were to buy them in isolation, as you don't need to time the market. A good plan will also benefit you, as it removes the headache of constantly having to decide what investments to buy.

Of course, you will experience ups and downs, but a diverse, smooth and constant strategy can offset the lows and give you better returns overall. You also tailor the plan to your chosen level of risk, so you never feel that you are out of your comfort zone.

Pound Cost Averaging is a slow and steady strategy. As Paul Emerson once said, 'Investing should be like watching paint dry or grass grow; if you want excitement, take $800 and go to Las Vegas'. Pound Cost Averaging works when you save a steady, regular sum, rather than blowing wads of cash at irregular intervals.

So that's the theory, but what are the consequences of saving? What if I told you that the more you saved, the greater your growth would become? My mum always told me that 'the more you put in, the more you get out', and, with saving, she was completely right!

I am a keen golfer; I've played since I was a child and absolutely love this sport. I'm also quite competitive, and love a challenge, as you saw when I told you about L'Etape Wales Dragon Ride. A few years ago, on a gorgeous summer's day, my best man Chris had come to visit from Singapore, so we decided to hit the golf course. We've played against each other on many occasions, but this time Chris suggested we add an additional competitive edge.

"I tell you what Charlie," Chris said, "Let's make this interesting, and play for money for a change." Now I like to be cautious with my money, so I suggested, "Ok, if we must; let's play for 10p a hole". Chris works in the world of investment banking, and much like their reputation is less cautious with his money than I am, so his response comes back; "Ok, we'll start at 10p a hole, but let's double it after each so it focuses the mind."

"That sounds like a good idea" I said, thinking that we were only playing for a few pence. "You'd better get your wallet Chris, I'm feeling lucky today!"

So, we teed off and we both put our 10p into an old golf cap, which we were using to collect the winnings. 10p didn't feel like a lot, so I didn't feel like this was going to be an expensive round of golf.

I won the first hole, but Chris took the second. The game was on! Thankfully, by the time we reached the halfway house and the ninth hole, I was winning. Whilst we had a quick break, I decided to look into the golf cap; I couldn't believe it; there was £25.60! But then I realised that meant that the next hole was going to cost me £51.20!

"Chris, are you sure you want to carry on playing for money?"

"Yes, why not? The total can't go that high, can it? I mean, we only started by putting a few pence into the hat!"

So, on we went. By the time we got to the 12th hole, can you guess what the total was? £204.80! This game was getting expensive, but the prospect of winning spurred me on. I wanted that hat full of cash!

It was at this point that the totals started to explode! We only had 4 holes left to play and by the time we'd finished, I could barely lift the hat! Can you imagine what the total amount was? By the 18th we were playing for £13,107.20 just for that hole! All from starting with 10p.

The moral of this story is not about playing for money, instead it exemplifies an important savings concept. Compound growth is where your money doesn't just grow, the growth actually increases by reinvesting any interest you make on your money. The effect of the growth on the growth on the growth over time makes a massive difference to how much your money increases. Just a couple of % a year might not sound like a lot, but that affect every year makes a huge difference in the future.

As an example, let's take two 20 year olds, Max and Sam. Both invest £56 per month, every month, until they reach the age of 65. The only difference is that Max receives a rate of 6% of his money and Sam receives 7% of her savings. Only a 1% difference, but take a look at the difference that makes:

| Max | Paying £56 per month until age 65 at a rate of 6% | Fund of £153,000 |
|-----|---------------------------------------------------|------------------|
| Sam | Paying £56 per month until age 65 at a rate of 7% | Fund of £212,000 |

That's a 39% difference! All from just 1% difference in the rate of return. It just shows how much a difference a couple of percent can make over the long-term.

Therefore, it's important to consider how you save, not just what you save. I would recommend that you start to think about getting a good rate of interest or growth in your money, that beats inflation. That way, you should be able to benefit from compound growth and reach your goals much quicker.

Time in the market is just as important as how you save. Stock Market 'players' still give me chills to this day. Pulling their hair out over whether it's a 'bull' or 'bear' market and spending countless hours trying to guess where the best profit can be made is downright exhausting, and, I believe, ultimately futile.

The very best way to be a successful investor is to firstly formulate a plan, and then patiently stick to it. Time in an investment is more important than trying to perfectly predict market fluctuations. If you look back to the Compound Growth and Pound Cost Averaging sections of this chapter, you will see why this is the case. Nobody, not even Warren Buffet, can accurately predict what the markets will do 100% of the time, or where their money will best perform. Those who tell you they can, are either on the last legs of their luck, or are lying.

What I always tell my clients is to practice a little patience. To succeed at investing you will not reach your goals overnight. You must wait. Ride out the ever-present, and sometimes volatile, peaks and troughs of the Stock Market and you should reap the rewards. The more time you can afford to do this, the better for you. Let's look at another example to illustrate this point:

Jennifer is 40 years old and has decided that she wants to retire at the age of 65. In those 25 years, she saves £100 per month into her diversified investment strategy. She exercises patience and doesn't panic buy when markets are shooting up; equally, she doesn't sell because it looks like the world is imploding! After 25 years, Jennifer has saved a total of £30,000, but because of investment growth, her account is worth £107,000!

Jennifer's nephew, Harry, sees what his aunt is doing and decides that he too wants to save in the same way. Harry is only 20 years old, but knows that he doesn't want to retire until he's 65 too. Having a lower income than Jennifer, he opts to save less than her per month, and settles on the figure of £56 per month, which by coincidence means he has also saved £30,000, the same as Jennifer.

What do you think Harry's total at age 65 would be? He's saving nearly half of what Jennifer is per month, but has 45 years in which to save rather than 25.

Harry's final sum at age 65 would be £153,000- £53,000 more than his aunt. It just goes to show why time in the market is so crucial; you don't need to save huge sums each month to reap significant rewards. The more time you have to save, the fatter your savings pouch will become. In short, don't wait until tomorrow; start saving now!

Sadly, it's at this point that many would-be investors lose their confidence. I mentioned earlier that investing gets bad press. The general feeling is that investing is far too risky and can completely decimate your hard-earned savings. I'm not going to tell you that this is a myth, as frankly, sometimes it can. That is, if you don't understand the rationale behind risk.

I want you to understand that there is no such thing as 'no risk'. If we look at that jar of coppers as an example, the amount of money you're collecting is being affected by risk every day. No, it's not directly Stock Market risk, but it's risk all the same.

The best analogy I can use here is chocolate. When I was a teenager in the 1990s, you used to be able to buy a Cadbury's 'Chomp' for 10 pence. If I went to buy that same bar of chocolate today, I'd be lucky to find it for less than 20 pence. Not only has it doubled in price, but it's actually shrunk in size: it costs more and you get less. What's happened here is inflation. The worth of my money has decreased, so I can buy less with it.

That jar of coppers will gradually become worth less and less as time progresses. It's not receiving a rate of interest, so it will never beat inflation. The same can be said for any money sat in the bank that is receiving a rate of interest lower than the rate of inflation: that can include your savings accounts, Cash ISAs, especially where the introductory offer has expired and at the time of writing, all current accounts.

As an example, at the point of writing, the best accessible Savings Account I can find on a comparison site is offering 1.1% interest per annum. The current rate of inflation on the goods you buy is 3.5%. This means that even if you have chased down a good savings account, you are guaranteed to lose 2.4% of your money every year this continues. Yes, you read that right, guaranteed to lose 2.4%. And whilst I accept this is a relatively high example, almost without exception you would have lost money every month for the past 10 years! If that had been the inflation and savings rate across that 10-year period, £10,000 of your savings would now only be worth £7,843!

As a caveat here, I would like to point out that it is generally a good idea to keep some money in cash for day-to-day
expenses and emergencies, so you certainly shouldn't be
thinking about investing all of your money, but more on
that in a later chapter!

So, you are always taking risk, but there are different
types. To receive growth, and allow Compound Growth
to work it's magic, you do need to take some pre-defined
risk with your savings. When it comes to your money, especially your saving strategy, you must feel confident and
secure that you are doing the right thing. A good Financial
Planner will conduct a Behavioural Risk Assessment before you invest, to understand your appetite towards risk,
as well as how much you can afford to lose. Before you
invest, make sure that you know your unique score.

Once this has been defined, you can then look at how
much you need to achieve to meet your goals. There are
a variety of tools and techniques, which I will cover in my
next book about planning your future. However, for now,
I just want you to understand that you need to calculate
your Financial Security Number (i.e. the amount you will
need to be able to reach the expenses for the rest of your
life) before you can begin to decide upon your level of
risk. Your Financial Security Number can be simply calcu-
lated as follows:

| **Expenditure** | (Passive Income i.e. rent) x 25 |

It is important to consider that with a Financial Security
Number, your income is almost irrelevant - it is your expenses that count. For example, if you earn £100,000 each

year you have a high income. But, if you spend £90,000 per year that money would not last very long.

The calculation provided here is by no means exact, but it will give you a good indication of what you should be aiming for. At Efficient Portfolio, we adopt a more sophisticated approach to calculating this number, using a tool called a Lifetime Cash-Flow Forecast, which illustrates the levels of wealth you will need to live out your unique goals. The Lifetime Cash-Flow Forecast enables us to hypothesise different scenarios and tailor expenditures on a year-by-year basis, rather than calculating how much you will need on a flat basis.

Once you have your assessment result and your Financial Security Number, you can work out if you can afford to take less risk to achieve your goals, or if you are comfortable in taking more. Generally speaking, the more risk you take, the higher the returns, but you can also often suffer the greatest losses. Remember, your investments should only be set at a risk level you are comfortable with. As Pound Cost Averaging shows, slow and steady can still win the race, if invested correctly.

To calculate how much risk you can afford to take yourself, you need to work on the premise that you will get an income from your investments plus inflation from your invested capital. For example, if you invest your money with a relatively high level of risk, and could expect a 5% rate of return plus inflation returns, then you need to multiply your figure by 20. If you are more cautious, therefore expect a rate of return of 3%, then you multiply by 33.

Over time your tolerance to risk will change. There will be periods in your life where you need to be more guarded with your wealth, and times when you can take more risk to build higher gains. Equally, market fluctuations will, over time, make the level of risk on your investment increase. In both scenarios, it is important to 'rebalance' your investment portfolio, so it never becomes more or less risky than you want it to be. In the 5th book in this series I will talk about the importance of reviewing your investments, but for now please understand that it is a habit that all successful investors follow, and is pivotal to you securing financial freedom and the future you want.

This is all quite complicated, so if you would like to learn more about this topic, you can download a copy of my first book, 'The Dream Retirement: How To Secure Your Money and Retire Happy' from here http://www.dream-retirement.com/book

**Pound Cost Averaging**

The best way to ensure that you don't need to time the market and are not paying over the odds for your investments. This slow and steady strategy of regular saving helps you to get more for your money and prevents 'impulse' investment purchases that are high risk.

**Compound Growth**

Growth on growth on growth, even by just a few percent each year, makes a huge impact upon your savings. Reinvesting the interest you accrue on your savings will help you to significantly grow your savings in a faster way, ensuring that you can achieve your goals and more!

**Time**

Time in the market will always beat timing the market. Plot out your goals, implement a strategy to achieve them and then practice some patience. The more time you have to invest, the better your results will be, so start saving now!

**Risk**

Investments are often regarded as high risk, where you could stand to lose everything. Monitoring and adapting your personal risk level will ensure that you only take the appropriate level of risk with your investments, so you feel confident and secure. You also need to periodically review your risk levels to ensure they are still relevant to you.

# The Money Management System

The previous chapter may have felt slightly technical; it was meant to! If you want to achieve your goals through your money, I feel that it is essential that you have a solid understanding of the strategies and factors that can help your wealth grow. But now you understand the rationale, just how and when should you save?

I see so many people grow physically uncomfortable when you talk to them about saving. But why are a huge proportion of the population petrified of putting money aside? The objections I hear usually sound something like this: "How can I save when I have bills to pay"; "I can't afford to save, because I don't have enough money"; "I'll never be able to retire, because I'll never have enough."

It is a common problem that many of us have too much month at the end of our money; we run out before our next pay day and are living 'hand to mouth'. What I'm going to

share with you now will help to put an end to that pre-
dicament for good, and help you to build a savings fund
that will empower you to fill your life with the things you
love. You'll be able to wave goodbye to your old mindset
towards saving and comfortably meet your expenses.

First of all, imagine that you are 70 years old. You've never
saved any money, so every weekday morning you must
get up, get in your practical, but slightly old, car and drive
to work. It's a beautiful day outside, but you have to miss
out on that and instead open the door to your grey, con-
crete office. You spend your days doing the same thing
you've done for 50 years, willing the hours away. Then,
at the end of a long shift, you come home to watch the
same TV programmes and eat the same meals you've
been consuming for as long as you can remember.

Suddenly the phone rings and it's your friend who retired
20 years ago. They tell you about their latest amazing trip
to Australia to see their grandkids. They are so excited
to tell you about the visit to Ayers Rock, how they volun-
teered at a koala sanctuary for the day and how tall their
grandchildren are becoming. They have to cut the call
short, because they're off out to the Sydney Opera House,
but wish you well and hope to see you soon.

How would that make you feel? Personally, it would make
me incredibly sad, jealous and feel generally down about
my life in comparison. I'd be happy for my friend, but wish
it was me making all those memories.

Now I want you to imagine a future where you are able
to retire early. You will be young enough and healthy
enough to fully enjoy the world's most incredible expe-

riences, rather than hearing about all the exciting adventures that your friends and family are having whilst you're still slogging it out at work.

You could be climbing a mountain, soaking up the sun on an Indonesian beach or tasting the most delicious food in the world's number one restaurant. Whatever ticks your Bucket List boxes is yours for the taking. You don't have to go to work; if you do, it's out of choice because you love your job. Instead, you make new memories every day, spend time with your loved ones and see the side of the world you'd always dreamed of.

How does that make you feel? I imagine, pretty good! I'd feel energised, fulfilled and downright elated that this life was mine.

So, which life are you going to choose? To save or not to save, is that really a question?

How can you achieve that lifestyle, but still meet your day to day expenses now? I believe that the most reliable way to have success with money is to have a system. And a simple one at that. My two daughters, who are currently aged 8 and 10, use this system, and have done so since they were 3 years old. If they can do it, there is no excuse for you not to.

The 'M' in 'SMART Savings System' stands for 'The Money Management System', and will change the way you view money forever, and the sooner you use it, the sooner you will reach financial security and be able to live out your dreams.

The truth is that most of these goals or dreams will require money. Let's face it, unless your best friend owns a private jet, if you want to travel you'll need money. Even if you crave a simpler lifestyle, without money you won't be able to stop work and focus on what's important to you.

Before we go any further, there is no point in aimlessly saving. We all need a degree of money in order to live the life that we do. At the end of the day, (unless you are 100% self-sufficient and live on your own island and do not have to pay for any services) we all have bills to pay, mouths to feed and costs to meet. Your Financial Security number is the figure that represents the sum you need in order to finance all of these costs. In short, the number reflects how much you need to earn or save in order to pay for the essentials. This becomes particularly relevant when you begin to consider retirement and how much you need to earn in order to support yourself and your family. Always bear this figure in mind- it is the minimum amount that you need to make. If you earn less than this number, your security could be at risk if you do not make any necessary changes.

Now we move on to you Financial Freedom Number. This and your Financial Security Number are closely connected, in the sense that they are unique to you and represent the sum that you need. However, your Financial Freedom Number is not about necessity, it focuses more on how much you need to realise your dreams. Many people focus on Financial Freedom as an exact figure, or a net worth, which they wish to achieve. There is a simple calculation that will give you this number:

## Your Income x 20

So, why exactly do you need to understand these numbers? Well, knowing your Financial Security and Financial Freedom Numbers will change your focus, drive and motivation for saving. People often say to me, I cannot afford to save, the same as they say they don't have the time to get fit. The problem is not about the time or the money, it's about the priority. It reminds me of a story.

A wise man asked a younger man to put as many stones into a glass jar as he could fit. After filling the jar to the brim, the wise man asked, "Is the jar full?". The young man replied "Yes, it is full." So, the wise man then gave him some pebbles and asked him to continue to add to the jar. After completing this task, the wise man again asked, "Is the jar full now?" The young man said, "Ok, now it is full." The wise man brings out a bag of sand, and again asks the young man to continue to fill the jar, this time with sand. After completing the task, the wise man again asked, "Is the jar full?" The young man replied, "Ok, now the jar is definitely full." So, the wise man picks up a jug of water, and pours it over the stones, pebbles and sand, until the jar is full.

The moral of this story is that you need to put the big rocks in your life into the jar first, then the pebbles and finally the sand and water; it is amazing how much you can fit into your jar when you try.

I am currently training for an ironman. That takes a lot of training every week. I can only ensure I train by putting my planned sessions into my diary first, and building the other aspects of my life around them. The same goes for money. If you want to have a financially free future, you need to build a system that delivers the important bits: the rocks first!

Now you've got a Financial Freedom Figure to aim for, you need to put into place a system to achieve this goal. And not just this one; you also need to include the many aspects of your life that are important to you between now and then. If all you do is save you'll have a dull life, so you need to reward yourself for your hard work too, but not at the expense of the bigger plan.

I'm a firm believer that the habit of saving is almost more important than the amount you save. The Money Management System encourages you to divide your money into categories, before any of it is spent. It doesn't matter whether you've got £1 per week pocket money (like my daughters) or £50,000 per month income, if you don't use this system, you'll find that you'll never have enough.

The Money Management System splits your income as follows:

| Specifics | 10% of your income |
|---|---|
| Incident | 10% of your income, or 3 month's expenditure |
| Medium Term | 10% of your income |

| Play Account | 10% of your income |
|---|---|
| Long-Term Growth | 10% of your income |
| Essentials | 50% of your income |

This system helps you to save for the future, whilst allowing you to meet your expenses and still enjoy life. In the next chapter I will show you how to create these accounts, so that the money ends up in the correct destination before you spend it, but for now I wanted to explain the areas in a little more depth.

## ⚙ Specifics

In terms of retirement, the 'Specifics' is almost the most important 'pot' for your money, as it will ultimately allow you to stop working. The money put into this account will form the basis for your savings into investments and could help you to earn enough passive income for your future. As you saw in the previous chapter, 'Rationale', the money you invest could benefit from compound growth and pound-cost averaging, and should ideally be invested into a diverse strategy that fits with your tolerance to risk. An example of where to save could be something like a Self-Invested Personal Pension or an ISA. The sooner you invest, the greater your chance of success.

## ⚙ Incident

Sadly, life has a way of often presenting us with emergencies and difficult times. You might lose your job, need a brand-new roof on your house, or pay out for a new boiler. Whatever the emergency, they are often unexpected, but that doesn't mean that you can't prepare for these testing events.

Everyone should have an emergency fund established before they think about investing for the medium term. A guide of how much is appropriate is usually considered to be 3-6 month's income or expenditure, or roughly 10% of your income.

## ⚙ Medium-Term Growth

Even the most frugal of us will have things in our lives that we need, but that tend to cost a fair amount of money. Examples of this might be a car, a new kitchen or a wedding. You may even argue that a holiday fits into this category, especially if it is for a special occasion like an anniversary. If you don't save for these very specific purchases, chances are that you won't be able to afford them. Putting money aside each month will help you to purchase items or pay for events that make a positive impact on your lives. I also get a real 'kick' out of saving for specifics, as I love to see my savings nudging closer to a set amount that will help me to improve my home or help my children life a better standard of life.

In this category also comes your savings towards your personal growth and development. I am a firm believer that if you're not growing, you're dying. It doesn't matter how old you are, personal development is crucial for mental health, happiness and a feeling of purpose in life. You can use your Medium-Growth Fund for training courses, seminars or materials to help you learn and grow. Investing in yourself can of course help you progress in your career, but it can also be for enjoyment. Retirees, in particular, often feel that they have no sense of purpose: they no longer work, or 'use their brains', so feel lost and useless. If you want to learn something, go and do it! Especially in retirement, as you finally have the time to learn and further your skills. You might have always wanted to learn how to mould clay into beautiful sculptures, or master Italian. Any type of learning is positive, so allow yourself to go on that course, purchase those books and learn from the experts.

## ⚙ Play Account

From time to time we all need to have fun! I'm not going to preach to you and say that you need to deprive yourself of the things you love in order to achieve your goals, because frankly you don't! As humans, there will always be things in life we don't need but want, and, if you save correctly, you can have them. For example, you might relish a night out with your friends, or wearing the latest 'must have' fashion item. For me, it's golfing equipment and gadgets, and for Caryl, my wife, it's new shoes! We don't need these things, but they help us to feel good.

A few years ago, I heard a story about a lady who earnt around £700 per month. Things were really tough for her, but she still followed a structure similar to The Money

Management System. Every month she'd put £10 into her 'Play Account', thinking that she really couldn't afford it, but did it all the same. Then, every month, she'd spend that £10 on something she loved: chocolate, a cinema ticket or admission to an art exhibition. Previously, she felt she couldn't afford to do these things, so her life was dull and boring, but as soon as she started to spend her 'Play Account', her outlook changed. She started to enjoy life and felt that she had a better connection with those around her. She felt more positive about her future and looked forward to her treat each month.

We work hard for our money, so it's important we get to enjoy it on a regular basis. Life can be tough and tedious at times, so injecting a little fun is so important. With this in mind, I urge you to spend your 'Play Account', at least quarterly- go on, you've earnt it!

## ⚙ Long-Term Growth

The next account is where you should save to make large and expensive purchases. This might be a new home, university fees for your children or maybe even something extravagant, like a boat you've always dreamed of owning. To enable you to meet these goals, investing could help to plump up your savings, but you should consider investing in something flexible, for example an ISA or a PIP (Personal Investment Portfolio), so that you can access the funds when you want to make that purchase. The Long-Term Growth account also helps to bolster your 'Freedom Fund', as the more money you put into your investments, the greater the effects of compound growth.

## ⚙ Essentials

Like death and taxes, some things in life are inescapable. We all need food, shelter and warmth, but sadly these things don't usually come for free. We all have costs and bills in our day-to-day lives, and paying for is a necessity. Rather than shirking bills, and praying that the next instalment will miraculously be less, you need to face up to your responsibilities and take control of your outgoings. By putting sufficient funds aside each month to cover these costs, your life will feel less stressful and you can have the peace of mind that your mortgage, gas bill and TV Licence are all covered in full.

This is our SIMPLE Money Management System that if you implement well will set you up for a financially free future. However, would you agree that there is more to a happy future than just the money? If you want to be truly happy, you may want to add two other accounts to make this the system of a true champion.

The SIMPLE Money Management System will ensure you have financial certainty, freedom and have a varied life with friends and loved ones; could there be any more? Well yes, there could. If you want to be truly happy, you need 2 more accounts. I am not going to suggest how much should go into each, or where you should take it out from, but I will say that once you have the basics sorted, the real key to your success will lie here. These 2 accounts turn The SIMPLE Money Management System into The SIMPLEST Money Management System!

## ⚙ Succeed

What do I mean by The Succeed Account? If you want to truly succeed in creating the life of your dreams, a life that leaves you feeling that you are achieving the best you can, you need to keeping learning and growing. Only when we feel that we are progressing in life, and developing as a person, can we feel truly happy. Whether this is books, audiobooks, seminars, post grad's or TED talks (if you don't know what these are visit http://www.efficient-portfolio.co.uk/contact-us/not-necessarily-financial/ to see some of the best).

Jim Rohn once said; "I can give you a guaranteed way to be wealthy beyond your dreams 25 years from now. That is to read 1 book a week between now and then." He's not talking about the latest Dan Brown thriller either. Personal development and business books will get you there, but putting money aside each month to give you clarity on ensuring you continue to grow will allow you to succeed in whatever you want to do. After all, if you are not growing, you are dying!

## ⚙ Tithing

Ok, so I was struggling for a word for this account that started with a T, but you could also call this the 'Contribute', 'Give' or 'Charity' account. Giving back can be incredibly rewarding, especially when the cause is close to your heart. In my business, I have created the Efficient Charitable Portfolio, which gives to numerous local and national charities each year. Each month, we give these charities a slice of our monthly earnings, not because I have to, but because I think it's important to help others. You may think that you don't have enough money to give anyway, but I guarantee by giving a small amount away to a more needy cause you will get 10 times more back in the future. If the principles are tithing are to be believed, what goes around, comes around, so giving back is a mutually beneficial act.

I want to set each of you a challenge: for one month, starting from when you get paid, I want you to put 7 jars in your house, each marked with one of the funds I've mentioned. I then want you to split your income as prescribed, and spend the money only as recommended. See how it makes you feel and, more importantly, see if you can afford to save.

# 4 Automate

Everything this book has taught you so far has given you the tools and know-how to save for your future. Following the steps and guidelines supplied in the previous pages, you will become a savings-sensei and have an incredible future ahead of you, filled with all of the things you love.

You will also need to bear in mind the psychology of saving. As I've already touched upon, the habit of saving is almost more important than how much you save. Regular, steady contributions will pay off, so you need to think of saving how you would brushing your teeth: it's something you do almost without thinking every day. You brush your teeth to make sure that they stay strong and healthy and keep you chewing for the rest of your life. Your savings also need to support you through the duration of your time on this planet, so make sure that they are also in the best condition possible.

But, does it feel a little like too much hard work? The reason so many people shy away from their finances is because they simply cannot be bothered to learn and implement the secrets of my trade. And please don't think that I'm berating you, if you are one of these individuals! Most people do not have the time or knowledge to make a success of their savings, so you shouldn't feel alone.

In fact, I've got a special gift specifically for you; the magic glue that binds the likes of Pound Cost Averaging, Compound Growth and the SIMPLE Money Management System all together.

As with the rest of their financial planning, the majority of people rarely commit to investing as much as they know they should; others may start to save, stop and fail to revisit their planning, and some people completely ignore the fact that they will need money for their future. The intention of many people is to start at the next pay rise, and yet they then rarely implement this. But my secret, which I'm about to share, will completely cut out the need to actively 'think' about your planning; instead, you can reap the rewards of saving without lifting a finger.

In the previous chapter I set you the 'jar challenge', where I asked you to create 7 pots to put your money into. That's all well and good, but wouldn't it be more effective if this process could be done automatically for you? Personally, I think electronic automation is the best way to ensure your Money Management System is a success: it removes the temptation to 'mess around' with the amounts, it's quick, easy and gives you a clear insight into just what is happening with your money. It also removes human errors, such as forgetting to pay bills or making impulsive, often regrettable, purchases.

We've all heard the phrase that 'money burns a hole in your pocket' and it's true! Regardless of your good intentions, if you've got £50 in your wallet, you will spend it, and probably not on what you should! By automating your money this problem is removed and you are setting yourself up for financial success. Not only that, but modern technologies allow you to monitor your balances, analyse your trends and have been proven to help you reach financial security much quicker.

For many people, especially the younger generation, starting a savings plan from scratch can feel overwhelming. Thankfully, in recent years, a plethora of digital money-tracking services and applications have emerged and with these new automated tools, you can start saving without thinking about it.

Even if 'apps' seem like a completely alien concept to you, many online banking providers allow you to replicate the 'jar' principle and create your very own accounts to divert your income before you spend it. Even at a base level, simply setting up, and regularly checking, Standing Orders to your chosen charities, investment firms and utility providers, will ensure that your money goes exactly where you intend it to, when you want it to.

We as consumers now have a wealth of options to choose from to take small steps toward financial freedom. It may seem daunting, but embracing technologies can be the difference between a bright tomorrow or a broke today.

If you are an employee, for example, saving for your retirement couldn't be easier. Now that auto-enrolment has become mandatory for nearly all UK business, your employer set up a suitable pension scheme for you and your colleagues. Whilst this is not the place to discuss the best types of pensions for you, this habit of regular saving is, without doubt, a beneficial addition to your savings and your future. Best of all, it will be automated from your salary, so you don't have to actively move money into your savings fund.

I recently read an interview on the CNBC website that illustrates the importance of automation so well that I wanted to share it with you.

---

*When Grant of Millennial Money looked at his bank balance after graduating from college, he knew he had to buckle down. With $2.26 to his name, he moved back in with his parents, landed a digital marketing job and started building websites on the side to complement his $50,000 salary. Within a year, Grant was making more money from his side gig than his full-time job.*

*"I was hooked and turned my side hustle into a digital agency that I still run today," the now 31-year-old, who goes by his first name exclusively, tells CNBC. "I've generated millions and millions of dollars in revenue growth across my clients."*

*While much of his financial success is due to the fact that he focused on earning and developing multiple*

streams of income, a key step to building wealth is saving, Grant says. During his five-year journey to millionaire
status, Grant saved 50% of his income. He didn't just save
a ton of money — he put it to work. After all, "in order to
build wealth you need to be making as much money as
possible on your money," Grant writes on his blog.

Today, despite his financial success, he still focuses
on living simply and sets aside 40% to 50% of what he
makes. The key to saving half your income, Grant says,
is to make things automatic: "Automation is essential.
When I first started saving and investing, I was a little
more old school — I was trying to invest as much as possible into the online savings accounts I had set up and
it was a pretty manual process. Now, one of the biggest
recommendations I make is to automate as much of
your savings as possible."

Today, there are a handful of apps and tools "that make
it so easy to save without even thinking about it," the self-
made millionaire says. He recommends talking to your
HR department and having a portion of your income automatically sent to a savings or investment account. This
is in addition to contributing to your 401(k), Grant notes.
You can also look into micro-investing apps that invest
your "spare change." Acorns, for example, will round up
your purchases to the nearest dollar and automatically
put any spare change to work.

Grant isn't the only one who advises putting your financial plan on auto-pilot. As self-made millionaire David
Bach writes in "The Automatic Millionaire," automating

*your finances is "the one step that virtually guarantees that you won't fail financially. … You'll never be tempted to skimp on savings because you won't even see the money going directly from your pay check to your savings accounts."*

*One of the reasons I love this story so much is that it alludes to one of my all-time favourite books 'The Automatic Millionaire'. It's a great read for anyone interested in creating their own money management system, but it also hammers home the concept of automation. In another of his books, Bach goes on to say, "What determines your wealth is not how much you make but how much you keep of what you make." With automation, you will be able to 'keep hold' of more of your money and not squander it unnecessarily.*

---

Whether it's your day-to-day household expenses, or the monthly contribution you make into your pension, always try to automate as much of your money as possible. Set up Standing Orders now, so that you don't have time to forget, change your mind or let life take over. It really will make your life simpler and fast-track you on the road to financial freedom.

# ⚙ ⑤ Tax

You've started saving, you're managing your money effectively and you even understand the magical factors that will make your wealth garden grow. I think you're an absolute rock star; by following the guidelines I've given you, you'll have a far greater chance of reaching financial freedom than the majority of the population. Take a moment to congratulate yourself and bask in your glory. You deserve it.

Now stop. I've got some bad news. Like all superheroes, you've got an enemy; there's a threatening villain hiding in the wings, hell-bent on undoing your good work and destroying everything you've done so far. And like a true nemesis, this cold-hearted menace is something you've known your whole life, and something that you can't escape.

Benjamin Franklin warned us when he said "In this world, nothing can be said to be certain, except death and taxes." You'll be pleased to know that I'm not going to take a morbid tone in this chapter; that comes later! Instead, I'm tackling one of the biggest threats to your financial freedom- tax.

Before we go any further, I want to make something very clear. As a UK citizen, especially one who works for their money, I accept my fate when it comes to tax. To evade it is illegal and immoral, so I am certainly not suggesting anything along these lines! To pay for the National Health Service, Police, Fire Brigade, State Schools, State Pensions and general upkeep of our country, we need to pay tax. It's an annoyance, but one of life's less likeable facts, and one I completely accept.

But what I do object to is over-paying tax on my savings. You work so hard to put money away for your future, to then suddenly have your hard-earned wealth decimated by tax doesn't seem fair, and I don't want you to just accept it.

To illustrate this point further, I want to share a story about a couple I heard about several years ago called Janet and John; if you've read my book 'The Dream Retirement', you may recall this tale.

Back in the 1970's, Janet and John both had £10,000 to invest. A great sum back then, and now, to kick start their Financial Freedom Funds. Both Janet and John had really good jobs, so earned wages that forced them to pay higher-rate tax (sadly unavoidable in their cases). Both had similar objectives, in that they wanted to put money away for their futures and both wanted to achieve around 5% interest at the same level of risk.

But there was one huge difference between them: Janet took advice from a financial professional and was encouraged to invest in a tax-efficient environment. Sensible Janet, not that I'm biased! John, however, thought that he was financially savvy, so didn't need anyone to tell him what to do with his money. Rather than getting on my soap box and preaching about the benefits of utilising a Financial Planner, I'll let the figures speak for themselves:

In 2010, this is what the savings of both Janet and John looked like:

| John | Original investment of £10,000 | Now worth £19,542.00 |
|------|-------------------------------|----------------------|
| Janet | Original investment of £10,000 | Now worth £70,399.00 |

That's quite a difference, I'm sure you'll agree! But why is there such a huge disparity between John's savings pot and Janet's? The answer is compound growth and tax.

John's savings have been subject to tax throughout his working life, meaning that at least 40% (he's a higher-rate taxpayer) of his growth has been taken away from him. The funds left behind have been less than Janet's, so the effect of compound growth has been reduced. Janet, however, having been invested in a tax-efficient haven, has not been penalised, so that the growth, on growth, on growth has skyrocketed, as there is simply more in the pot to play with.

Imagine a piece of paper that is 0.05mm thick. If you folded this in half 50 times you would reach 100 million kilometres high. That's the equivalent of the Earth's surface to the moon! This is compound growth and is what Janet experienced. John, however, 'folded his paper' to then have the tax-man partially unfold it; John still achieved growth, but not at the same rate as Janet, and he sadly never made it the moon.

We'll come back to Janet and John shortly, but firstly I want to introduce you to your allies. If tax is the enemy, then these four superstars must be in your arsenal if you want to win the financial freedom fight. You see, you don't have to pay tax on all of your savings; in fact, there are some incredible ways of minimising your tax, giving you a much plumper pot of money for the future, which will see the effects of compound growth in much greater way. I.e. you'll reach the moon and not be left drifting in space.

When it comes to saving, you have four friends on your side. They are:

- Pensions
- ISAs
- Sophisticated Investments (EIS, SEIS and VCTs)
- Offshore Bonds

I'm going to explore each of these in turn, as they can all be a beneficial part of your savings strategy.

## ⚙ Pensions

How would you like to reduce the amount of tax you pay on your savings, and even be given a whole chunk of your savings completely tax free? Sounds good, doesn't it? So, let's start with a familiar friend that I'd guess you've all heard of. Pensions must be part of your savings strategy. I'm not talking about just the State Pension, which will hopefully still exist when you retire, but about pensions you actively save into.

Back in 2006, the pension landscape was so complex that the Government were forced to step in. They introduced 'Pension Simplification' as a measure to curb some of the complexities and make saving into pensions far more accessible and comprehensible for the general public. Over the next few years, 'Pension Freedom' was introduced, which finally gave people more choice over when and how they take their pensions, whilst rewarding them for leaving money in there. The only downside to all of these changes is that, whilst making these 'tax wrappers' even more attractive, they reigned in the limits on how much you could save and also have in there.

I don't want to bombard you with legislation, history or intricate detail, but it is important that you understand how attractive the 'Pension Wrapper' really is. When you get paid, you pay Income Tax of 20%, 40% or 45%, depending on your earnings. If instead of taking all of that money, you put some of it straight into the pension, you get that tax back. So, for £100 you put into your pension, it only actually costs you £80 if you are a basic rate tax payer, and £60 if you are a higher rate tax payer. That means you can get to financial freedom much quicker! Not only do you have more money in your account, there is more money there for compound growth to work it's magic on!

The money in a pension can then grow virtually tax-free, so it is exposed to even more compound growth instead of handing 20% or 40% of your growth to the government. Double savings! This is why John had a lower valued savings pot than Janet: John was charged for putting money into his savings fund at his higher-rate of tax, thus reducing the final amount. Janet, however, saved into a pension, so her money grew tax-free.

When you reach your retirement age, the earliest being 55 depending on your age, you can start to access this pension account. You can have 25% back tax free, and the remainder you can take as quickly or as slowing as you want, but you'll pay tax on that portion. Generally, most people earn less in retirement, so they are usually paying a lower level of tax at this time of their life, so herein is your third tax saving! You do not need to buy an annuity as historically you might. This is where you hand over all your savings in exchange for a guaranteed income for life. Sounds like a sensible idea, and sometimes it can be if you've only just saved enough, but for the last few years the rates have been so poor that most people have not bothered and have chosen to leave the money invested and draw an income from that instead.

This means that Janet's £70,399 pension pot is not quite accurate. In reality, this is what would've happened:

Janet took 25% tax free, so £17,599, which is nearly as much as John's total pot of £19,542! Janet used to be a higher-rate tax payer, but now she's retired, she's a basic-rate tax payer. This means that rather than the remaining £52,799 in her pension being reduced to £31,679, it equates to £42,239- still much higher than John's £19,542!

With pensions, you will need to pay tax at some point, but you are given the flexibility of paying this tax when you are at your lowest marginal rate. You can also take 25% completely tax free and benefit from tax-free growth. These really are the most effective tax wrappers for saving for the long term. Beware though, not all pensions are equal. They have a bad press because many are rubbish! Not all hoovers are a Dyson, and not all pensions deliver you good value, but the tax wrapper itself is a thing of beauty when saving for the long term.

The final benefit, in terms of tax for pensions, is what happens when you die. Pensions, on the whole, are Inheritance Tax friendly. If you die after your pension age, your beneficiaries can take the tax-free 25% of your pension Inheritance Tax free, as long as you haven't already taken it. With the rest of the money still in your pot, if you are under the age of 75 upon death, your beneficiaries can take this tax free, as long as they take it within two years. If you are over 75, the remainder of the pot will be taxed at the recipients Income Tax rate, and will often be less than the usual 40% Inheritance Tax they would have to pay if the money were in your estate rather than your pension. Quadruple tax saving!

## ⚙ ISAs

If Pensions are about deferring tax until later in life, ISAs are about saving tax later in life. The ideal retirement scenario is that you end up with a lump saving in pensions and an additional proportion of your money outside of pensions. As I've mentioned, pensions are fantastic for boosting your growth and potentially reducing the amount of tax you pay, but they do only defer the issue of tax. What you need to compliment pensions is a mechanism that allows you to withdraw money completely tax free, as well as give you access during your working life in case the need arises.

Next on our list of tax-savings heroes is ISAs (or Individual Savings Accounts to give them their full, but never used, name). ISAs do not offer tax-relief at the outset, but they are tax-free when you want to take money out. Utilising both pensions and ISAs in retirement will enable you to reduce the overall amount of tax you pay, and fund all of the things you love. You have the option with ISAs of investing your money in cash or in stocks and shares; you can also take money out as and when you need to.

Taking money tax-free sounds too good to be true; why wouldn't you just put all of your money into ISAs? The Government understand this, so sadly there is a cap on how much you can invest into an ISA each tax year. Furthermore, pensions are actually more tax-efficient in the long-term, that is unless tax rates go up. With ISAs, you pay the tax now and none later, whereas Pensions defer the tax to a later stage in life. At the time of writing, the allowance is set at £20,000, but it increases each year. For most people, especially those just starting out on their savings journey, this limit will be sufficient, but what if you want to save more than the allowance, or have a large windfall or savings account?

One strategy is to open a Personal Investment Portfolio (PIP). You will pay some tax on the growth you receive on these types of investments, but it will be capital growth, which is taxed through the Capital Gain Tax (CGT) regime. Very few people use up their Capital Gains Tax allowance each year, so most growth will still remain tax-free. The other benefit is if you don't utilise your full ISA allowance in a future year, you can transfer the funds from the PIP into the ISA to benefit from tax-free growth and will be tax free when you take the funds from the ISA.

## ⚙ Sophisticated Investments

For many people, using a blend of pensions, PIPs and ISAs will be sufficient, especially if you are relatively new to saving. But what happens once you have built a strong savings foundation, and your funds are exceeding the given allowances you are permitted on ISAs and Pensions, your PIP is starting to be charged CGT, or you are earning sufficient to be restricted on these allowances?

The following three strategies are somewhat the 'rebels' of the tax-savings heroes. They really are not for everyone, and can be very risky. I would not ordinarily recommend these types of investment to everyone, given their potentially volatile temperaments, but they could be worth considering if you have surplus wealth or are looking for some additional tax-efficient savings strategies. If you are considering them, you really must seek expert advice from an adviser who has specialist experience of these types of investments!

The Enterprise Investment Scheme (EIS) and it's cousin the Seed Enterprise Investment Scheme (SEIS) are investments in unlisted companies. Their close friend, the Venture Capital Trust (VCT) is a portfolio of investments in unlisted companies. All three offer very attractive Income Tax breaks, similar to a pension, however unlike pensions they can also help to defer or eliminate Capital Gains Tax and Inheritance Tax depending on which ones you pick, and you can access the money before 55.

They really are very tax efficient, but that is because they offer much more investment risk. This type of investment and tax planning is sophisticated and should not be taken lightly. I personally deal with these type of investments for some of my clients, and have seen some fantastic results, but, as I've mentioned, there is a large amount of risk involved. If you are keen to explore EIS, SEIS or VCT further, I'd love to talk to you directly, as I don't want you to run the risk of losing your capital! My email address is hello@efficientportfolio.co.uk or you can call my office on 01572 898060.

## ⚙ Offshore Bonds

If sophisticated investments sound a little too risky for you and would take you out of your comfort zone, there is an alternative. Again, I would suggest that this strategy only be considered once you've maximised your ISAs and Pensions and have a good 'unwrapped' or direct portfolio established that is using up your Capital Gains Tax allowance, but it is certainly worth considering as a part of your tax-efficient savings strategy.

Your final 'freedom fighter' is the exotic one of the bunch: The Offshore Bond. Whenever I talk about offshore investing, I tend to come up with a lot of resistance. The words 'tax' and 'offshore' often conjure up images of duplicitous playboys, surreptitiously secreting their wealth aboard yachts to evade tax. That is not what I'm suggesting!

If someone calls you out of the blue to recommend an 'irresistible' investment opportunity in the Cayman Islands, slam that phone down! If something sounds too good to be true, it probably is. These types of schemes are often fraudulent, unregulated and will burn your capital to dust.

What I'm talking about are legal, ethical and reliable Offshore Bonds that the FCA can oversee. A trusted and regulated Financial Planner will have access to them and will be able to recommend if they are suitable to your needs.

The reason I talk about them is because they can be very tax efficient. Offshore Bonds, unlike other bonds, don't lock your money in for a set time. Whilst you cannot claim income tax back like the pension, the money you pay in is subject to tax-free growth, and there is no restriction on access.

Offshore Bonds grow tax-free and you are able to take up to 5% of the amount invested as a tax deferred income, so no liability at that point. When the bond is surrendered, you die, or you exceed the 5% allowance, the withdrawals will be added back into the final total, and it is then you will need to pay tax at your Income Tax rate at the time, so bonds can offer you a degree of flexibility. So these are another great way to defer tax to a later stage in life when your income will be less. There are also some attractive options that allow you to gift part or all of it to your children or grandchildren, so that the growth is taxed against them.

Offshore Bonds are great if you are looking to draw an income from a longer-term investment, be that now if you are in retirement, or in the future if you are considering our retirement planning. If inheritance and estate planning are also concerns, using Trusts with Offshore Bonds can also offer a way to minimise the tax your beneficiaries would need to pay in the future, but you'll need to get specific advice on that, as this can be a complex area.

Tax is inescapable, but it doesn't mean that it needs to damage your savings. By utilising a blend of ISAs, pensions or alternative investments options, you can save or defer tax and give your savings a far great chance at growth. Ultimately, the more you have saved, the more of your goals you will be able to complete, and the more enriched your life can become.

Tax is complicated, hence why there are so many tax-specialists still in work. If you don't feel completely confident in what you're doing, the tax savings you make could end up costing you your capital, so it's prudent to seek help.

I'm one of those tax specialists (I promise you I'm not a dull character though); if you would like to talk to someone about how you can minimise the tax you pay on your savings, please do get in touch.

# Safeguard

"We cannot change the cards we're dealt, just how we play the hand".

Everything you do in life is a gamble. Nothing, apart from death and taxes, is guaranteed and you can never really know what is lurking around the corner. If you choose to walk to work without an umbrella, it might rain; if you book a flight to your dream location, it might get cancelled; if you get married, it might end in divorce.

I don't believe in crystal balls and Tarot cards. I don't think that any of us can accurately predict what will happen in our futures. But, despite not knowing, uncertainty is not a barrier to us humans; if it was, we'd never do anything! The lack of foresight shouldn't be an obstacle that stands in your way of living your life to the fullest. But that doesn't mean that we shouldn't consider life's unexpected moments and protect ourselves from the unknown.

A quick question: How many of you insure your cars? I would hope that all of you who drive do! I bet you even insure your homes, pets, mobile telephones, and even your holidays. We insure these things to protect them from the worst. Insurance means that if our kitchen caught fire, we'd have money to repair it; if our faithful four-legged friend broke their tail, we could afford to pay the vet to restore them to full health; if our holiday was cancelled, we wouldn't be out of pocket.

So why is it that so many of us neglect to insure the most important aspects of our lives? We seem to protect material objects and possessions, but forget about our health and income. We roll the dice everyday, and our fate is out of our hands. But so many people ignore this fact and do nothing to protect themselves, so let's look at this closely. If you earn £20,000 per annum at the age of 20, without pay rises other than those to match inflation you will, on average, earn over £1.85m during your lifetime. If you owned anything else that was worth £1.85m, would you want to insure it? If you were buying a house worth £1.85m, you want to make sure you had insurance in place before you owned it, because you wouldn't want to risk £1.85m even for one weekend, or one minute for that matter. So why don't you insure yourself? Because you are invincible? Are you sure? What could it cost you or your loved ones if you are wrong?

If you want to prepare yourself for financial freedom and security, there is a crucial element that millions of people neglect: Safeguarding your wealth. When I talk to my clients, there is one message that I repeat over and over again: "Protection is the most important aspect of financial planning, as you can never fully control what lies ahead. We can build you an amazing financial plan that will deliver financial freedom in the future, but only if life keeps going as it is. If something unexpected happens on that journey, it will derail your plan. Do you really want to roll the dice with something so important?"

When I talk about protecting your financial future, I'm really talking about safeguarding yourself in four key areas, subject of course to your own specific circumstances, so that you aren't rolling the dice with achieving your plan!

- ✹ Death
- ✹ Illness
- ✹ Credit (Mortgages and significant debts)
- ✹ Employment (Income)

There certainly are things that we can do to minimise the risks these foes present, such as healthy eating, exercise, paying off your debts and creating a lucrative and stable income, but ultimately, you never know. You could get hit by a bus, you could be made redundant, your business could fail, and your good intentions to repay debt could become impossible.

Before I go deeper into this subject, there is an elephant in the room that I want to address. Do insurances actually pay out? You've all seen the PPI miss-selling fiasco, and there are always stories of insurances not paying out, so is it really worth it? The key here is only to look at policies that are underwritten at the point of application, not at the point of claim. There is no point in paying for a policy that won't pay out when you need it. For our clients, we only look at policies that are fully underwritten before they take a penny off you. This excludes policies like Accident & Sickness and also Unemployment Policies. If you want the former, read on, as there are better ways to achieve this. If you really want the latter, you'll have to take the gamble with underwriting at the point of claim, but read the terms carefully. Either way, what I am going to talk about here excludes these policies, as they can be problematic in terms of paying out.

A few years ago, I met a couple in their early forties called Bob and Maria- I've changed the names here to protect their identities. They ran a successful, but relatively small business together, where they didn't have any employees- they did everything themselves. Bob and Maria were in good health: They were reasonably fit, didn't smoke and had three young children.

Tragically, Maria was diagnosed with late stage breast cancer. This came completely out of the blue and seriously rocked their seemingly steady boat. Whilst Maria was recovering, Bob had to completely take over the business; this was of course stressful for him, but meant that the company could keep afloat.

But life has a funny way of testing us. Just when you think that you've hit rock bottom, the ground beneath you opens up to show you the abyss. And that's what happened. Almost one month after Maria's diagnosis and treatment, Bob had a serious bike accident smashing his shoulder. There was no permanent damage, but it meant that he needed to take some time off work too. Thankfully, Bob had some basic Income Protection in place on his earnings, which gave them a little financial stability in these stormy times, but not nearly enough. This threatened to shatter their lives, personally and financially.

I'm pleased to say that both Bob and Maria made full recoveries, and are still clients and friends of mine today, but speaking to them afterwards, Bob admitted to lying awake each night wondering how he was going to pay their mortgage, put food on the table for their children, pay Maria's medical bills and keep the business afloat. They lacked the protection to ensure that their financial plan wouldn't be derailed.

It was an awful, frightening and eye-opening period of their lives. But what this episode showed them was the importance of ensuring there is a backup plan. If they had had some safety nets in place, life would have felt far more secure for both of them. They would have had peace of mind that they were still financially secure, and could have focussed solely on getting better, rather than worrying about money.

I didn't share that story to scare you. I wanted to just highlight how unexpected life can be. We don't know what lies ahead, but that doesn't mean we can't protect ourselves against the worst.

So, what can you do?

# ⚙ Death

Let's bite the bullet and get the worse case scenario out of the way first. Death only affects those left behind. Despite being one of the only certainties in life, none of us really want to think about it. But come out of your comfort zone and face this fact now. When you die, your loved ones will be the people left behind. What would happen to your family if you suddenly died tomorrow? Would they cope? Would they be able to live out all of their hopes and dreams? Or would they struggle financially? Obviously, they would be affected from an emotional point of view, but how would it affect them financially?

**Security**: Without question, being a parent has made me realise that I am not the most important person in my life. Giving my kids security and the hope of a bright future is what gets me out of bed in the morning. I fight to succeed everyday so that my children can have a great life. But what if I suddenly wasn't there? I wouldn't want my untimely death to scupper my daughters' futures.

Would your family still have financial security if you passed away today? It's not a nice thought, but one that you really need to consider.

**Stability**: In addition to providing financial support for day-to-day costs, such as food and bills, I'm sure that you would also want your family to sustain the same standard of living after you've gone. You hear horror stories of families having to sell their homes and possessions in order to get by after they lose a loved one. I'm sure this is the last thing you'd want for your family. Sadly, my best friend from university is no longer with us. When he left us as a result of a plane crash, he left a business behind too. A business that had his family coming out of retirement, moving the length of the country, as well as being out of pocket. Think about how your passing would impact those around you, and how much that might cost.

**Legacy**: In my book 'The Dream Retirement', I talked quite extensively about leaving a legacy, which is another consideration you should make. Part of that is leaving an inheritance behind for your loved ones, so that they can buy their first home, set up their own business, pay off their debts or simply to give them peace of mind that they won't suffer financially when you've gone.

Financial security, peace of mind, an inheritance or just certainty that bills can be paid, are all legacies we'd like to leave behind for our loved ones. A Life Insurance Policy can help to deliver all of these things, so it is a pivotal part of your financial planning strategy. How much you need will depend on your age, wealth and circumstances, but, generally speaking, as a good rule of thumb, you will probably need twenty-five times your income. Why so much? If you earn £20,000, a lump sum of £500,000 will generate a sustainable income of around £20,000 per annum for your loved ones.

Death is of course the worst case situation, but it is something that will happen to us all. Insuring your life will make the lives of your loved ones far more stable after you've gone, and enable them to carry on and thrive despite this difficult time.

# ⚙ Illness

The chances of you dropping down dead tomorrow are relatively small. It's not impossible, and the impact could be huge on your family, but the chances are still slim. Sadly, it's far more likely though that you could be diagnosed with a critical or even terminal illness.

According to 'Contractor Weekly', 'a recent study has revealed that one in two people born after 1960 will be diagnosed with some form of cancer during their lifetime.' These are frightening figures, but those statistics don't even take into account other life-threatening illnesses that could have a seriously detrimental effect on your finances.

If you are diagnosed with a critical illness, chances are that you would not be able to work for a significant period. If your salary sustains your family, can you imagine what this would do? They might not be able to pay the mortgage, meet household costs and would generally struggle to get by. Yes, you may be entitled to some form of statutory sick pay, but would this be enough? If you're self-employed, this problem is compounded even further: If you don't work, you don't earn any money.

If you think back to Bob and Maria, with both parties off sick, their business was at risk of going under and they had sleepless nights, worrying about how they were going to pay their bills. A Critical Illness Policy would have given them security and peace of mind: They would have been given a lump sum to pay off the mortgage or front some heavy capital costs at the point of illness, allowing them to focus on getting well.

Many illnesses require specialist treatments, home modifications or professional care, all of which can be very expensive. Say for example that you needed to build a downstairs wet-room, as you could no longer use the stairs. The cost of this would run into the thousands, but would be necessary for you to continue to lead a comfortable standard of living. You may have money put aside to cover this expense, but would you really want to spend your long-term savings on this modification, when it was originally designed to generate your Financial Freedom?

The beauty of Critical Illness Cover is that the payout is tax free and you can spend it on what you need to, whether that is medical bills, your mortgage or home modifications. You are also free to invest the money, so you can build a passive income for your loved ones in the years to come. In other words, Critical Illness Cover will give you a lifeline at this demanding and difficult time. You won't need to worry about the financial implications of your illness, and will instead be able to focus on getting better.

## ⚙ Credit

Unless you have been incredibly fortunate in life, chances are that you will own some form of debt. The biggest debt most of us have are our mortgages. Without this debt, we wouldn't be able to live in our homes, or provide a secure environment for our families, but it still can be a burden on our loved ones if we find ourselves in situation where we can't pay it.

I often hear people say that "debt dies with us". There is some truth in this statement, but it sadly doesn't apply to mortgages. If you die, and your surviving spouse, or other beneficiary, cannot pay, the bank will take the property, sell it, often at an incredibly low price, and use the money to pay off the outstanding mortgage. This leaves your loved ones with nothing: no home, and no legacy.

The same applies if you are still alive but have become incapacitated due to illness. Say you had been diagnosed with a rare form of cancer that renders you unable to work. You have Critical Illness Cover, so have received a payout, but now have to choose whether you pay for specialist treatment or pay your mortgage. It's an impossible decision, and one that you shouldn't have to tackle if you are seriously ill.

Whatever the reason for you being unable to pay your mortgage, the outcome is the same: You could lose your home, your security and your quality of life. Both you and your loved ones could suffer and find yourselves without a roof over your heads.

A simple solution for this is Mortgage Protection, which would payout the remaining balance of your mortgage in the event of death or serious illness. Imagine what paying off your mortgage could do in a time of need? You would be free from the worry of paying off this massive debt, and the crippling effect that losing your home would bring. The stability and security of knowing your home was not at risk would give you an immense sense of peace of mind, and allow you to focus on securing the other elements of your life.

I see many people with this that pays out only on death, because the critical illness element is more expensive. Think again if that is you. I'll stress again, suffering a critical illness is more expensive than dying. Dying leads to loss of income and a funeral, suffering a critical illness means a loss of your income, maybe a loss of your spouse's income so that it can assist you, the cost of medical treatment, adapting your house, recuperation, so as well as being more likely, it's also more costly. For me, financial planning is a must. Not just because I have 2 daughters and a wife that are dependent on me, but also because if I am critically ill, I am here and I need the money!

## ⚙ Employment

Like most people, I use my income to pay for my essential costs: food, bills and my mortgage. I also use my income to generate savings for my future, which will ultimately give me and my family future financial security. But what if my employment income was suddenly out of my control? What if it stopped?

In the last 5 years, the UK economy has been turbulent. With Brexit on the horizon, many companies are worrying what the future will hold and whether or not they will be able to keep their doors open for business. There is a huge feeling of unrest in the workplace, and job security is becoming weaker by the day.

Whilst redundancy is one problem, which I'm not tackling here, what if you couldn't work because of injury or illness? Statutory Sick Pay only stretches so far, and what if you couldn't return to work for months, even years? You'd still have costs, but no way of paying them. Critical illness cover deals with the immediate costs, but that would soon run out if you lost your income for a number of years, or even permanently!

What would you do if you suddenly found yourself in this situation? Could you and your family pay your bills? If you are the main-bread winner this problem is intensified, as suddenly you may not have enough for your family to survive on. Selling up and moving house at a time of serious illness would add to problems, not to mention derail your financial plan for the future!

Another consideration to take into account is your earning capacity. When we talk about building wealth, we often forget about how this is done. Ultimately, it is down to your income generation that will help you to save for the future, but what would happen if your earning capacity was taken away? If you are faced with the inability to work due to illness, suddenly your ability to build wealth is taken away and your future could be at risk.

My wife, Caryl, runs her own company, doing something she loves: gourmet cookery demonstrations. Owing to the success of my business, and my capacity to build wealth, Caryl can be very selective about when she works: she chooses what hours she puts in and has full flexibility to look after our girls in the best way possible. But sadly, if I was suddenly unable to work, Caryl's income would scarcely cover our mortgage, let alone anything else. She would then be faced with becoming the main-earner, which would completely change her and our family's lives.

Without a guaranteed income, most people would suffer. Even if you have ample savings, these would soon deplete if you didn't have an income, and the younger you are the worse this becomes. This is where Income Protection can offer you a beacon of hope.

Income Protection is a powerful product for anyone who wants to cover their salary so that they don't fall behind on their monthly outgoings. It also gives you peace of mind if you have dependents who rely on you. A few employers offer this type of protection, but they are relatively few and far between, so if not, you need to do this personally.

The real benefit is that you don't need to fall down dead or be diagnosed with a life threatening illness for your Income Protection to pay out a tax-free monthly income. This steady stream of money, often around 65% of your earnings but tax free, will give you a much needed helping hand in your time of need and allow you to get back on your feet.

## ⚙ Putting Them All Together

At this point you may be thinking that safeguarding yourself, and your wealth, is important, but do you really need everything I've spoken about. Very much like your household insurances, the protection I've spoken about covers different scenarios and will give you support at different points in your life. Your existing wealth will have a huge impact upon which protection you need, but ultimately, all four safety nets I've mentioned could work together to form a cohesive protection strategy.

Let's imagine the worst case scenario: you've been diagnosed with cancer. The policies you have in place may vary in when and how they pay out, but this is how they could all work together to provide you and your family with security:

**Income Protection**: Owing to your illness you can no longer work. Your Income Protection Policy will pay out around 65% of your income each month, so that you can still pay the bills and put food on the table. The money you receive will mean that your quality of life is not compromised and you can still choose to live the lifestyle that you value.

**Mortgage Protection**: The burden of your outstanding mortgage will be removed, meaning that your monthly income won't be overly stretched and your family have the security of knowing that the family home is safe. You won't lose your home at this difficult time, so you will have peace of mind and your family can draw on this asset, either for capital or inheritance, in the future.

**Critical Illness Cover**: Your cancer, or other illness, may require specialist treatment that isn't covered by the NHS, so with this policy, you'll have the choice to pay for it. You can also pay for any necessary home adaptations or even take a nice cruise to recover properly. If any of this money is left over, you are free to invest it into your savings strategy for your family's future, to keep your financial plan on track.

**Life Insurance**: If the worst does happen and you pass away, the sum received by your family can be used to support them for the rest of their lives, easing the burden of your passing. Thanks to the Mortgage Protection, they won't need to spend this on your outstanding debt, and can instead use the money to give them security and income for their futures.

Of course, this is an extreme example, but there are plenty where you'll need just one policy. But which one? For example, if you put your back out, you'll need your income protection to help you, as you won't die or suffer a critical illness as a result, but you may still have a substantial amount of time off work.

Nobody wants to think about what life would be like without the security your wealth and income can bring, but it's vital that you do. You can't predict what the future will hold, but you can try to limit the ill effects that illness or death will have on your own and your family's lives. Protecting yourself against the unexpected will mean that all of your hard-earned savings won't be decimated if the worst happens, and you can continue to enjoy the fruits of your labour. You cannot put a price on security, but a protection strategy is certainly as close as you can get.

Life is like walking a tightrope: Don't do it without a safety net!

If you are concerned about protection, I would always recommend speaking to an expert who can assess your specific needs. There is no point in paying for something you don't need or not putting into place something that could prove to be a lifeline. My firm, Efficient Portfolio, can certainly help with this. Call the office on 01572 898060 or email hello@efficientportfolio.co.uk and the team would be happy to talk you through your options.

# 7 Bringing It All Together

Well that's it, you've done it; you've prepared for your future and graduated from my SMART Saving Solution school.

Taking that first step towards financial freedom is one of the scariest, but bravest and most rewarding things you will ever do when it comes to your money and your future. Putting in place the building blocks for success will help you to reap the rewards of your hard work for many years to come, and the knowledge you've learnt can be passed onto your children and your friends, so that they too can start to prepare for their futures.

Now that you've learnt about the SMART Saving Solution, you will be able to retire early enough to enjoy amazing experiences with your friends and family, rather than listening to their stories of freedom while you are still at work. You've learnt everything from creating a saving-mindset and maximising your savings through compound growth, right through to the Money Management System and understanding how to reduce the amount of tax you pay on your savings.

But, like all good stories, this is only the beginning. Saving, and all the tricks and techniques associated with it, are the cornerstones to your success, but there is so much more to cover if you want to succeed.

At the outset of this book, I told you how I have discovered that there are really 6 key areas that need to be mastered if you want to create a financially free future. Whether you call that retirement, or your life 2.0 (the enhanced version of your life), unless you take control of your financial future, you will be working until the day you die.

Some people enjoy what they do for a living, and never want to give up, but is that you? If it is, wouldn't it more enjoyable still if you knew that working was a choice, and that you didn't have to if you didn't want to? Most people want to either stop work in the future, or at least have the choice to. But to be able to do that you need to create financial freedom or enough capital that you can live off for the rest of your life.

That's why we created The Efficient Money Method. This is our unique system that helps people plan for a financially fit, happy and healthy future.

You've now completed the first step in that process, 'Prepare', so you've got five more areas to master to become financially free.

# ⚙ PLAN

The second area we need to master to create a financially free future is to plan. Probably the biggest concern people have in the lead up to retirement is that they will run out of money later on in life. Either that or they stop themselves doing the things they want to, thus ending up as the richest man in the graveyard. The key to a successful retirement is being able to look into the future, see what you need, and then plan how you can get there, including what you can afford today.

This aspect in particular is the key to having peace of mind in your financial life. Without it, you will feel uncertain and worried about what the future holds. With it, you will have the confidence to live the life you want.

We created **The SAFE Retirement Roadmap**, so that we can help our clients clarify what their financial future looks like, and help to forecast different scenarios, because this gives them the confidence to make the right financial decisions for their desired future. Can you imagine the empowerment that clearly knowing about your financial future would give you?

**The SAFE Retirement Roadmap** gives you confidence, so that you can afford to do your bucket list at a time when you are able to, rather than leave it too late when it's no longer an option. It gives you the ability to make the right decisions today by allowing you to see future implications. And finally, it allows you to make wiser decisions with your planning strategies, to really maximise how hard your money works for you.

**The SAFE Retirement Roadmap** will give you the peace of mind you need by helping you **plan** for a financially happy future.

## ⚙ PROFIT

The third area that you need to understand, to create your Life 2.0, is **profit**. Saving money is important, but if you do not get that money working harder for you, then you will have to save twice as much and it will run out twice as quickly. To combat this, we need to allow your savings to generate **profit**. What I mean by this is that you've got to get your money growing, but not just any growth; growth over and above inflation. Only at this point do you start to **profit**.

This is an area where I believe big insurance companies have really let so many people down. There are too many products out there that provide very low or non-existent growth; even some of the more sophisticated solutions that attract high fees, and have 'gold branded' names, let you down drastically in this area. Sadly, so many encourage you to take too much risk, and more risk than is needed to get the returns you require.

We created **The RADICAL Investment Approach** so that our clients could be confident that they were getting the best returns possible, without taking more risk than is necessary or they are comfortable with. We ensure client's money is growing over and above inflation, but without gradually getting riskier and riskier, as usually happens naturally in a portfolio.

**The RADICAL Investment Approach** gives you the control so that you can ensure you are getting the right level of returns you need, with a level of risk you are comfortable with. This means you always know your money is in the right place, as opposed to gradually taking more risk than you should be. It also ensures you avoid the investments that are likely to blow up your financial plan.

**The RADICAL Investment Approach** will ensure you get your money working for you as hard as possible, thus delivering your real **profit** for the future.

## ⚙ PENSION

The fourth area you need to conquer if you are going to create a financially free future is your **pension**. So, what does that actually mean? As and when you reach the point where you want to stop work, we need to find ways to turn the capital you've saved into an income you can live off for the rest of your life. That is your **pension**.

The choices you have available to you at this stage can be confusing and daunting, but also can make the difference between a broke or a brilliant retirement. You could of course hand all those savings over to one company in exchange for a low but guaranteed income for the rest of your life, but these annuities assume you are as likely to climb Kilimanjaro at 95, as you are at 65. We all know that is unlikely to be the case, and most people want to spend more at the start of retirement than they do towards the end. The old way of creating a pension also meant that if you don't live long into retirement, you would miss out on your hard-earned savings. That just doesn't seem right.

In order to help our clients at this stage in their life, we created **The DREAM Income Strategy** to ensure that they maximise their hard-fought savings and turn them into a flexible, dynamic income that can deliver what they want, when they want it.

As an example, I had a client who had been forced to retire early. He was extremely upset when we first met him, because, whilst being forced into early retirement was not his fault, he was sure he had let his family down. He had not saved enough or in the right way to create the retirement he had promised his family. He was upset that their retirement would not be the later life he had envisaged and he was worried that they would run out of money as they grew older.

Using the tools and systems in **The DREAM Income Strategy** we were able to show him how to maximise his savings, so that he could create the later life he wanted, he could deliver on the promises he had made, and he and his family would have the confidence to enjoy that later life.

**The DREAM income strategy** can give you the choice of how much income you need for that particular year, which means you can draw what you need without paying more tax than you need to, and still do all those amazing things you've dreamed of. Most of our industry tries to create a flat and rigid income strategy, which leaves you unable to do what you want when you want to. **The DREAM income strategy** will help you turn your hard-earned savings into a fluid and accessible **pension**, which will facilitate your own 'dream retirement'.

# ⚙ PROGRESS

Everything I have been through so far has been about getting your finances into the right position for you now; but would you agree that things change? Legislation changes, the market changes, your situation changes, and all this affects the effectiveness of your planning. That's why if you want to continue to have a financially free future, you need to continually **progress** forward. You need your financial planning to evolve with you, rather than stagnate as all too often is the case.

So, if we give you a clear plan, get your money growing and create you the best income strategy, that will be great today, however, by this time next year, it could be wrong. There will be changes that mean you need to make adjustments to ensure your financial planning continues to support your unique situation.

And this is the area our industry is really bad at. Much of our industry only wants to see you again if they think they can sell you something else. For those that do see you, generally they focus on the basic investment performance and nothing more. But a proper review process needs to be so much more than that, to ensure you actually **progress**.

That's why we developed **The Progressive Review Programme**. This is unique to us, and is why many clients leave their current financial adviser to join us. We deliver a review service like no other, in ways that allow us to do so much more to ensure your financial planning actually does evolve with you, in time effective ways for you and us.

**The Progressive Review Programme** ensures that you are still **preparing** for your later life in the best way and that your money is still generating the most profit possible. By reviewing your finances on a regular basis, we can make sure you aren't taking more risk than is appropriate to your situation, but also taking enough to get the returns you need. The programme helps you to remain in touch with your plan, and your **pension** Income, and allows you to maximise the opportunities that life presents.

**The Progressive Review Programme** will allow you to feel comfortable and give you the peace of mind that you are **progressing** towards or through your Life 2.0.

## ⚙ PERSONAL

Would you agree that there is more to a happy retirement than just the money? What I found after many years of helping people plan the financial side of retirement, was that they would also worry about how they would spend their time and how they would remain fit, healthy and happy. These factors are as just as important as the money. If you want to truly create your own dream retirement, the final piece of the jigsaw is to control the **personal** side of your retirement.

I regularly see clients who are approaching retirement who are far more worried about what they will do after they have stopped work than their money. They also worry about becoming a shadow of their former self and withering away soon after stopping work.

That's why we created **The Fulfilled Life Formula** so that you can really maximise your time in retirement. Using **The Fulfilled Life Formula** we help our clients design their time, so that it is filled with purpose and passion. We help them define their bucket list, so they have reasons to live and things to look forward to, and we help them dramatically improve their health.

**The Fulfilled Life Formula** doesn't just focus of the health of your body either, but also the health of your mind and of your relationships. It will allow you to leave a legacy rather than just a Will for your loved ones. Something that will outlive you and be there for generations to come.

**The Fulfilled Life Formula** will help you leave a legacy rather than a liability by helping you to create by design the **personal** side of retirement.

**If** you would like to see how The Efficient Money Method could work for you, please get in touch on 01572 898060 or email hello@efficientportfolio.co.uk today.

# Prior Preparation Really Does Prevent Poor Performance

You'll remember that I'm a farmer's son and spent my youth helping my dad cultivate his crop. For those who aren't familiar with the agricultural life, the farming community is very close-knit and, as such, farmers are always paying close attention to what their peers are up to. It's a little like having several nosey, but well-meaning, neighbours constantly twitching their curtains!

When I was still a boy, I remember my father telling me a story that has stuck with me until this day. The tale is about two farmers, who were in constant, but healthy, competition with each other. They were always peeking over their neighbour's fence to see what the other was up to. This parable really struck a chord with me, so I would like to share it with you now.

There were once two farmers called John and Graham, who owned neighbouring farms. John was a rather rotund, rosy cheeked fellow, who loved nothing more than his wife's homemade pies and a pint or two of local ale by the fire. Graham, a slightly reserved and quiet chap, was more 'outdoorsy', rose before the birds every morning and prided himself on being strong, resilient and hard-working. Despite being friends, and both relying on their crops to make a living, the two men were polar opposites. Whilst John liked to relax and take life at a slower pace, Graham could never settle and was always on the go.

Anyone who has known a British summer will tell you that it's the perfect environment for growing crops: a mix of sun and rain, which changes like the wind, but keeps the ground fertile and rich. But this summer was very different, because this summer a drought struck.

The once lush and verdant lands owned by John and Graham became parched, burnt and arid. The crops were wilting in the hot sun, like the hopes of the two farmers for a successful harvest.

On one particularly hot day, John was sitting in his garden, drinking a tall, cold glass of lemonade. He didn't see the point in farming today, as the blistering sun would undo all of his efforts. The sun was making him feel lethargic and unmotivated, so he decided that he'd just spend the day in the shade of his favourite willow tree.

John kicked off his shoes and stretched his arms up high. As he did, he turned his head and saw his neighbour, Graham, bright red in the face and dripping with sweat.

"What on Earth are you up to?" shouted John.

"I'm building a dam." replied Graham.

"Why bother? It's as dry as the desert out here. There's no water!" scoffed John

"The rain will come, you'll see." warned Graham.

"Stupid man" thought John. "Why waste a day like this working, when you could just soak up the sun and relax."

The drought continued for three more days, each hotter than the last. Every day, Graham woke at the crack of dawn, donned his Wellington Boots and grabbed his spade. He spent ten hours digging and building before returning home, exhausted from his efforts.

On the fourth day, bored of just lounging in the shade, John strode over to his neighbour's fence to watch Graham at work.

"Are you still building that ruddy dam" shouted John.

"No" said Graham, "I've finished the dam, so I'm building an irrigation system now."

"Heavens above" exclaimed John, "You'll put yourself in an early grave with all that digging and lifting! Why don't you come and join me for a nice, cold beer instead?"

"Thanks John, but I'd better get on. The rain's coming." replied Graham.

"He gets stranger and stranger" thought John. "Who'd turn down a refreshing beer on a day like today? We've not had any rain for nearly two weeks now. What's the point?"

Two days later, everything changed. The sky turned dark grey and the air became heavy with the promise of a storm. And then it came: a deluge of rain from the skies that finally quenched the crops' thirst.

"Ah finally, the rain's come" thought John. "Tomorrow I'll get back to work and tend to my fields."

And the next day John did just that. But the rain had stopped and the hot sun had returned, so by midday, John had had enough.

"It's ruddy hot today" shouted John over his neighbour's fence.

"I know" agreed Graham. "It's supposed to be like this for another two weeks."

The ferocious sun continued to beat down on both farmers' lands for the next fourteen days. All of John's crops became as dry as paper and crumbled into dust. He wouldn't be able to harvest anything this year, which meant that winter would be bleak for him and his family.

John couldn't face telling his wife what had happened, so he solemnly paced his garden, hoping to find the right words. As he reached his neighbour's fence, he stole a glance over at Graham's crops.

He couldn't believe his eyes. Instead of the bone dry, dead land that belonged to John, Graham's land was thick with bright green plants, thriving despite the sun.

"It's just not fair" thought John. "How does he always get all the luck?"

John and Graham had the exact same tools at their disposal, but the difference was preparation. Whilst John rested on his laurels and prayed that nature would take care of his problems, Graham took matters into his own hands. By building his dam and irrigation system, Graham ensured that his crops were cared for in the tough times ahead. And it paid off. Whilst John's crops withered and died, Graham was able to keep his plants fed and watered, so that they could grow into a successful harvest for him and his family.

I'm sure I don't need to tell you the moral of this tale. By preparing, Graham built a solid foundation for his crops to grow, which delivered him an abundant harvest year after year.

You might not be farmers, but that doesn't mean that you can't prepare your land for future success. The tools I've shared with you in this book will keep your crops watered for years to come, so that your yield can flourish and provide you with plenty for your future.

If you do nothing else, I urge you to now go and build your own money management system and look at the best places to save your wealth, so that it continues to grow. I also strongly encourage you to protect what you have; so that life's unexpected events don't derail or damage what you've worked so hard to create.

But what else should you and Graham do next? Preparation is the bedrock of your success, but it's only just the starting point. Your savings, protection and money management strategies are only the start if you want to be financially free. What are you going to do with your harvest now it's grown? How are you going to know what you need for the future? And how will you know which decisions are wise and which should be avoided?

Have you ever tried to get somewhere without a map, or, in today's world, a Sat Nav? Road signs and prior knowledge are valuable, but sadly can be inaccurate, out of date or completely wrong! By aimlessly trying to find your way on your own, you are actually preventing yourself from enjoying the journey, arriving on time or even getting there at all.

Now that you've got the tools, you need to keep them sharp and try to anticipate what impact your actions will have.

In the next book, 'The SAFE Roadmap: Clearing the Path to Security', I will show you something that will change your life.

Imagine being able to clarify and shape your future, so that you clearly understand what impact your actions today will do to your tomorrow? I will show you how to make wise financial decisions that will empower you to enjoy your life, whilst making sure that your money is still working hard for you. I will give you the skills and confidence to know what you need to do to have a bright, secure and happy future.

I can't wait to share this knowledge with you, and help you start out on the path to clarity and security. But, if you can't wait until then, why not get in touch? I'd love to hear about your experiences with the SMART Savings System and how your life has changed since you've started to prepare for your future.

Or maybe you'd like me to help you build a strategy? My expert team and I at Efficient Portfolio specialise in helping people to build, manage and protect their wealth. We offer an innovative approach, designed to put you and your individual goals at the centre of everything we do.

Whether you'd like to share your story, or would like our help, feel free to reach out to us by emailing hello@efficientportfolio.co.uk, calling 01572 898060 or visiting www.efficientportfolio.co.uk

We can't wait to hear from you.

Until next time.

Charlie.

# About the Authors

## Charlie Reading APFS

Charlie Reading is a Chartered Financial Planner, entrepreneur, speaker and author that has a passion for amazing retirement planning. Amongst his 4 businesses he runs the successful Chartered Financial planning practice Efficient Portfolio that specialises in investment and retirement planning and is based in both Rutland and London. Having been in the Financial Services industry since 1999, his qualifications place him in the top 10% of all financial advisers in the UK, with particular focus on investment management, wealth protection and retirement strategies.

Charlie was previously a financial adviser with 2 of the largest firm of independent advisers in the UK, but he realised that these companies were too product focused and weren't directing their attention to the client's true needs and concerns. When he set up Efficient Portfolio he wanted to change the focus to a more client centric truly independent approach so that he could deliver much more value to his client's financial future. He does this using innovative tools like Lifetime Cash Flow Forecasts.

Charlie has successfully helped many people save for, manage and enjoy their retirement, often when they didn't think they had saved enough. Through careful planning he has shown them how they can maximise the money, reduce their risk and design an income strategy that delivers the life they desire. But Charlie is also passionate about building a better life through understanding what makes us happy and healthy. What makes our mind tick, and what strengthens our relationships, because ultimately the financial side of retirement is just the starting point.

He loves spending time with his wife and two daughters, playing golf and squash, cycling, travelling and is passionate about scuba diving, safari and good wine.

# Charlotte Colton

Charlotte Colton is the Practice and Marketing Manager for Efficient Portfolio. After graduating from Kings College London, with a degree in English Language and Literature, Charlotte has worked as an Assistant Banqueting Manager and also undertook a Graduate Scheme in Business Management, which honed her skills in marketing, management and delivering exceptional service to clients. After this, she developed her financial knowledge within the Savings Department of Barclays Bank.

Originally from Rutland, Charlotte has recently moved back to the area after studying and working in both London and Liverpool. Charlotte manages all aspects of the marketing and events for Efficient Portfolio; implementing marketing strategies, organising and running events and ensuring that the team continue to provide a high level of customer service for our clients. She has co-authored this book with Charlie to offer a unique stance on personal finance, particularly for career-driven women who are new to financial planning and looking for a fresh approach.

Away from work, Charlotte enjoys travelling and experiencing new cultures, experimenting in the kitchen, yoga, running and the theatre. She spends the majority of her time at home looking after (chasing after!) her two bull-dogs, Napoleon and Hector. She is also a keen writer, both professionally and in her spare time.

27663782R00066

Printed in Great Britain
by Amazon